Boley
Oklahoma's Famous Black Town

Boley
Oklahoma's Famous Black Town
James Shaw Sr.

Copyright © 2012 by James Shaw Sr.
ISBN 978-0-578-09722-0
Published by
YES PUBLISHING GROUP, YWHOIAM, LLC
1208 SE 16th Street
Moore, Oklahoma 73160
www.ywhoiam.com/ypg.html
All rights reserved. No portion of this book may be reproduced, stored in a retrieval system, or transmitted in any form or by any means – electronic, mechanical, photocopy, recording, scanning, or other – except for brief quotations in critical reviews or articles, without the prior written permission of the author or publisher.

Dedication

The book is dedicated to James and Zylphia Bowler, my grandparents and pioneers to the great town in which I was born and raised. Another dedication goes to Jimmie L. and John Hope Franklin, two of history's greatest historians.

Contents

Dedication		v
Introduction	The Teachings of James Bowler	ix
Chapter 1	Boley Beginnings	1
Chapter 2	The Black Ideology behind Boley's Success	15
Chapter 3	Boley in Print	43
Chapter 4	My Family	55
Chapter 5	Boley after Statehood	65
Chapter 6	Sand Creek Community and Boley Education	69
Chapter 7	The Turbulent Times in Boley	83
Chapter 8	Special Note on Julius Rosenwald	89
Chapter 9	Conclusion: Boley Today	93
Bibliography		99

Introduction

The Teachings of James Bowler

"I walked with just my shoes and the clothes I had on. I made a place for me in this land. It's a big accomplishment for a son of former slaves." – James Bowler, my grandfather, 1942.

James Bowler was one of the most well-to-do residents of Boley, Oklahoma. He owned several acres of land and was able to live comfortably with his wife Zylphia in Boley's countryside. The irony is that Bowler arrived in Boley after walking for days from Bossier Park, Louisiana with virtually nothing. He didn't have much except a dream and a zest to work. James and Zylphia were among the earliest residents of Boley. They were also my grandparents who raised me in this thriving all-black town.

Boley was, and still is, one of the predominately black towns in the state of Oklahoma. In its prime, it was the home of over 7,000 citizens by 1911 (Hamilton, 1991). By this time, it was deemed the largest Black town in America, which was a major accomplishment considering this was only four years after Jim Crow laws were put on the books and Oklahoma gained statehood. Booker T. Washington himself once commented on the great condition of Boley and referred to the town as a "tribute to the negro race" (Washington, 1908). Other prominent Black leaders followed suit when they heard about Boley's success. Boley would be not only the home to several landmarks, but the location of a bank robbery gone wrong by the infamous criminal, Pretty Boy Floyd.

To many, Boley would simply represent a period in history long gone. However, Boley holds a special place for me in my life. It was the place where I was raised and where my family made a better life for themselves. In this work, I will give a history of the place that was one of the largest and most successful all-black towns in America and discuss my family history as well. This research started several years ago as a result of several factors, including the aging of my great-aunt Clarissa (who will be 95 this year) and a family reunion that was held in Oklahoma City two years ago.

This writing will chronicle Boley from its infancy, while the state of Oklahoma was just Indian Territory; through its golden years during the late 19th to early 20th century; to its present in the early 21st century.

Chapter 1
Boley Beginnings

Black presence in modern-day Oklahoma did not originate with the Black settlers from the South. The first documented occurrence of people of African descent dates back to the sixteenth century when many of them accompanied Francisco De Coronado and other Spanish explorers to the area on a gold-seeking expedition through the territory. They came as either fellow explorers or slaves, though in some cases they were considered both. Estevanico, or Esteban, was one of the first people of African descent documented to be in Indian Territory (Taylor, 1998).

Contrary to popular belief, the slaves and mixed bloods who came with the Five Civilized Tribes were not the original African descendants to have arrived here. On the other hand, one can argue that the largest migration of Blacks occurred during Indian Removal.

Journey to the West

The American Civil War officially ended in 1865, but the aftermath of war proved to be disastrous for freed slaves. Many had to endure the perils of racism brought on by those pro-Slavery Whites still seething from their defeat at the hands of the Union North. The Southern Reconstruction began as an event that would prove to be helpful to former slaves as it included the creation of the Freedmen's Bureau and the occurrence of Blacks gaining offices in Congress in the late 1860s through the early 1890s.

The Ku Klux Klan was disbanded by several government forces just years after its creation because of its reign of terror and the lasting impact it left on daily life for the newly freed slaves (Taylor, 1998). Nevertheless, seeing former slaves and pre-slavery free Blacks holding public office and gaining help from the government further angered Southern Whites, and therefore a push for the re-enactment of Black Codes prevailed.

Laws such as the Grandfather Clause would soon follow as well as continued mistreatment at the hands of hostile Whites. As a result, many Blacks made the very first Great Migration North and West.

Photo: Main Street of Boley
Credit: Our Boley Picture Book

Boley came to be as the result of a bet wagered by W.H. Boley, the leader of Fort Smith and Western Railroad Company, and attorney Lake Moore. The bet was centered on whether "negros" could prosper on their own and handle self-governance. The men were on different sides of the debate: Boley in favor of negro self-governance, Moore on the other. A common stereotype of the time period - the idea that Blacks were too "primitive" to behave in "civilized" society and that they needed to be dependent on Whites - was fresh. Society was moving into the 21st century, but the Jim Crow mentality still lingered and became even stronger after statehood (Franklin, 1982).

Boley was created on land originally allotted to James Barnett for his daughter Abigail. James Barnett was a Creek Freedman who came to Oklahoma during the Indian Removal Period with the Muscogee Creek Nation from what is present-day Georgia. After removal, Creeks as well as other tribes that were forcibly removed to Indian Territory were made to live on allotted lands known as reservations. For the first few years, they were subjected to inhumane living conditions. Life for the former slaves was ten times worse, especially since the tribes brought slavery back with them. It is important to note, however, that the same attitude was not shared by all of the tribal people. Some Indians treated the Freedmen with respect and saw them as equals before and after removal.

The government allotted lands to the Indians when they arrived in Indian Territory and Freedmen were among the people who received them. Creek Freedmen were a group of former slaves of the Muscogee Creek Nation. The Creeks - along with the Cherokee, Chickasaw, and Choctaw tribes - owned slaves. These tribes in particular saw the adoption of this "unusual" institution as a step closer to becoming "civilized," as defined by White society (Katz, 1996). Slavery, however, would not save them from the wrath of those who believed in Manifest Destiny. There were several influential Blacks who came with the Natives to Indian Territory. One such person was a man named Silas Jefferson, who became known as Ho-tul-ko-micco, or "Wind Clan chief" in the Creek Nation (Zellar, 2005).

Photo: Silas Jefferson
Credit: Oklahoma Historical Society

Despite evidence from the Dawes Rolls that all of the Five Civilized Tribes had Freedmen, in reality only four of the Five Civilized Tribes actually owned slaves. The Seminoles were widely known to harbor runaways, not own them. The runaways lived with them freely on their lands and enjoyed trading with outside forces. They were major players in the Seminole Wars. This was true of my wife Lena's ancestor Abraham, an African Seminole Leader, and John Horse, the founder of the all-Black and Indian town Wewoka, now the site of the capital of the Seminole Nation.

Abraham of the Seminoles

Whether they were actual "slave owners" or not, all of the Five Civilized Tribes had Freedmen rolls and most of their Freedmen were given land allotments. James Barnett was one of them.

Barnett was a widowed Creek Freedman of Choctaw/African descent who was brought to the area with the Creeks. He was able to receive deeds for four separate allotments for his children; he wanted all of them to live nearby each other in order to keep his family close together.

Barnett, like several other Freedmen, was able to sell his land. The same was not true for their Indian counterparts; the government would not allow Native Americans to sell their lands. However, an official amendment in the Dawes Act stated that if any "land that is adjacent to railroad stations, the only exception would be a forty-acre homestead" (Hamilton, 1991), so with this knowledge, Barnett knew that he could get a good rate of his daughter's land since it met that condition.

The land that Boley and Moore wanted for their project just happened to belong to Abigail Barnett, the six year old daughter of James. The interest in Abigail's land arose from the fact that it was located just adjacent to the Fort Smith and Western Railroad, the company for which Mr. Boley worked. Fort Smith and Western Railroad was founded in the late 19th century, and in the early 1900s it was opened between Guthrie and Fort Smith, Arkansas.

Even though she technically owned this land, her father was deemed the overseer because she was still a minor. Therefore, Boley and Moore had to obtain permission from Abigail's father as well as the Department of the Interior. Barnett was glad to get the land off of his hands because "the land could be used for nothing else," not even a farm (Hamilton, 1991).

Barnett received $100 dollars per year for five years and was happy with his decision to allow it to become a

Black settlement. After obtaining full rights to the land, Boley and Moore knew they needed to find a reliable town manager. Boley suggested his good friend Mr. Thomas M. Haynes, a Black man.

Mr. Haynes was not highly educated and, to some, would have seemed an unlikely choice. However, he proved himself worthy of the job. A native Texan, he was an excellent town manager during his tenure as well as a successful entrepreneur. Even though Boley, Haynes, and Moore are credited as the founders of Boley, James and his daughter Abigail should be included in that title (Hamilton, 1991).

The early months of settlement in Boley proved to be rough for some of the new residents. Many had to live in poor conditions and opportunities for employment nearby were limited. This brought several close to poverty. Fortunately, this phase did not last long and many were able to come out of this condition quickly. A year after Boley's establishment, the town began to thrive.

Haynes once compared Boley to "the pyramids of Egypt," noting an "imperishable attestation of the power, might, and intellectual genius of a race" (Crockett, 1979). This was a true testament to Boley's potential. Boley also provided another choice for those new Black settlers coming into Indian Territory. Langston City was around at the time, but it did not provide a railroad station.

Photo: The T.M. Haynes building as it stands today

Boley's residents exhibited such town pride and respect for one another that it showed when the town encountered problems from outsiders. The earliest instance of such trouble came from Creeks as well as their Freedmen who were virtually neighbors of the Boleyites. They were called "Watchinas" and "State-Raised Blacks" by the locals. Rising tensions developed between the two groups because the Indian Freedmen saw these new Black settlers as intruders on their lands despite the fact that the land was purchased from one of their own.

Early Black settlers and Indians faced several problems with one another at first, but eventually there was an attempt to join forces with the Indian governments in order to create a "Black-Red coalition." This would ensure that Indian Territory would become a Black and Indian Mecca under the rule of both groups and finally provide a home for them. Edward P. ("E.P.") McCabe was instrumental in this effort by promoting the new idea of Oklahoma becoming an official "Black" state (Crockett, 1979).

This strongly suggests that the state of Oklahoma may very well have become an all-Black state since it also contained more all-Black towns than any other state in America.

The plan to officially name Oklahoma the "All-Black State" actually started with talks of making the former Indian Territory just this. Indeed, Senator Henry W. Blair of New Hampshire introduced a bill in favor of the proposal. Other early Black towns in the United States include Nicodemus, Mound Bayou, Fort Mose, Rosewood, Freedmen's Town, and others that had been founded before Boley.

The "father of the Black towns," exoduster E. P. McCabe is not mentioned much in Western scholarship, but his influence is stapled in the Western African-American diaspora. McCabe, a New Yorker by birth but a Westerner in occupation, was successful in politics at a young age. He was poor in his early years but worked hard to gain success. Even though he had to cease his education after his father's death, he took a job in order to support his family.

Photo: E.P. McCabe
Credit: Oklahoma Historical Archives

Through his job on Wall Street, he became a notable land promoter in the West, attempting to lure former slaves from the South to the new Black settlements. In the same year as the infamous "Land Run," McCabe helped lead a campaign to make Indian Territory an all-Black state. He hoped that by achieving such a feat, he would also become the governor of the new state with his city, Langston City (home of the only HBCU in Oklahoma, Langston University), as its capitol. This idea was supported by several officials, and McCabe attempted to convince President Theodore Roosevelt to jump on the bandwagon. Another tactic McCabe hoped to use was to "settle several Black majorities in each Oklahoma Territory election district" (Crockett, 1979). This in turn would ensure that each district would vote in favor of a Black state.

These feats show that McCabe was not only an icon in the Black Western expansion, but an important figure in Oklahoma in general. McCabe's interest in helping Blacks relocate to the West was genuine; he put their interests and well-being before his own. He would put his image on the line in order to make sure that Blacks experienced prosperity during that great migration West.

Despite the success of Langston City (known today simply as Langston) and other towns he promoted, McCabe's attempt to lobby support for the governorship failed. The Freedmen's Oklahoma Immigration Association was founded on March 15, 1881 to help colonize thousands of Black Freedmen in Oklahoma Territory. But any hopes of a large Black migration were dashed when Secretary of the Interior Samuel J. Kirkwood asked the commissioner of the general land office, Curtis W. Holdcomb, to review whether, and to what extent, Black Freedmen had rights to settle in the Oklahoma Territory (Crockett, 1979).

After statehood, McCabe also lost his political position. He filed a lawsuit in order to "overturn the segregation of railroad passengers" (Littlefield, 1973). Disgusted with the outcome, McCabe and his wife relocated to the Midwestern city of Chicago where he passed away at the age of 70 without a dime to his name. Despite these shortcomings, E.P. McCabe will always be known as an icon in the movement for Black prosperity and survival in the post-slavery years.

In the time between 1890 and 1910, over thirty Black communities were formed in Oklahoma. This resulted in the territory's Black population rising to over 130,000. Boley itself had over 2,000 inhabitants by 1908. After each detail was ironed out, Boley, Creek Nation, Indian Territory was officially founded in August of 1903 as one of Oklahoma's newest towns.

Photo: Booker T. Washington and Boley
Credit: Our Boley Picture Book)

When Dr. Booker T. Washington came to Boley, he was truly amazed at the progress that he witnessed there. Dr. Washington was a great orator and educator who founded Tuskegee Institute, now known as Tuskegee University. He once called Boley "the largest and best Negro town in the world." Booker T. Washington was especially proud of this town mainly because he had endured such hardship as a child growing up in slavery.

Another reason Dr. Washington found the town so appealing was that he knew many of the town's residents were just like him – former slaves who had traveled North and West for better opportunities.

Here is a portion of what he had to say about Boley in his article: "In 1905, when I visited Indian Territory, Boley was little more than a name. It was started in 1903. At the present time it is a thriving town of 2,500 inhabitants, with two banks, two cotton gins, a newspaper, a hotel, and a 'college,' the Creek-Seminole College and Agricultural Institute" (Washington, 1908).

The Boley Post Office was founded just one year after the town's establishment, and Mr. L. Mimms was the first postmaster. Mimms had an interesting, trademark manner of delivering the mail: carrying it around in his hat. He also allowed stores to call in when they were ready for their mail to be delivered.

BOLEY'S INCORPORATION

IN THE UNITED STATES COURT FOR THE INDIAN TERRITORY, WESTERN DISTRICT, AT WEWOKA.

In re the Incorporation of the Town of Boley. } Petition for Incorporation.

To the Hon. Louis Sulzbacher, Judge of the United States Court for the Western District of the Indian Territory:

The undersigned inhabitants and qualified voters of the town of Boley, Western District of the Indian Territory, respectfully represent unto your honor, that there are more than two hundred bona fide inhabitants in the town of Boley, and that there are more than twenty qualified voters in said town; that the Fort Smith and Western Railroad runs through said town, and has station grounds, and that said town has the prospect of becoming a good town of several hundred inhabitants in the near future; that the people of said town are desirous of having the same incorporated as provided by law, and desire the incorporate limits of said town to include the following described lands, to-wit: the south half of the south east quarter of section twenty and the north half of the north east quarter of section twenty nine, all in township twelve north, range eight east (S 1/2 of S.E.1/4 Sec.20 and N1/2 of N.E.1/4 Sec.29, T.12 N. R.8 E.), and annexes hereto an accurate map or plat thereof; that the name proposed for said Incorporated Town is "Boley"; that your petitioners name Thomas M. Haynes, Henry C. Cavil and Hilliard Taylor as their agents to prosecute this petition, with full power and authority to act in the premises and do all things necessary to be done in and about the incorporation of said town.

Wherefore your petitioners pray that your honor take the necessary steps to incorporate and make the necessary orders and decrees for that purpose and they will in duty bound ever pray.

Snapshot of Boley's Incorporation letter
Credit: Boley Our Town Picture Book

Chapter 2
The Black Ideology behind Boley's Success

Photo: Boleyites
Credit: Our Boley Picture Book

Several people have wondered how Boley continued to prosper as much as it did after enduring so many hardships during the early stages of its establishment. The question could be answered through several possible scenarios. One common explanation is the Black ideology that many of her residents possessed. This is the reason why several Black towns were able to weather great adversity. These predominately Black enclaves came as a direct result of Jim Crow practices of the South. Being freed from bondage was only one step in gaining complete and total freedom however. Blacks were aware that emancipation had not solved their problems entirely.

Early KKK members.
Credit: Library of Congress

Increased terror was on the rise in the South brought on by the hands of the disgruntled racist Whites who were still seething from the defeat of the Civil War. The founding of the Ku Klux Klan in 1866 was a direct result of this. Even with the passage of Civil Rights Act of 1871 which would disgruntle the KKK at its birth, violence against Blacks was still on the rise.

By 1877, Blacks were virtually disenfranchised with Black politicians losing seats and greater restrictions being placed on voting laws. The late 19th century in the South proved to be treacherous so the natural reaction for many free Blacks would be to find a place where they be comfortable and safe from these hostile acts.

Not all Blacks who lived in these predominantly Black towns were anti-White. Nor did all of them wish to reject the remnants of White society. They wanted a life of prosperity and to achieve this goal, they needed to work towards it and demand to be treated as equals. They displayed a level of endurance that was unlike what the rest of the White world was used to.

Establishing predominantly Black communities not only gave them a sense of independence, it also provided a new solution for a comfortable life. Indian Territory's White law enforcement more than likely would have ignored the complaints of the citizens of the Black towns. As a result of this unfortunate reality, the Black citizens created their own law enforcement with individuals such as Bass Reeves and Ike Rogers in leadership.

Photo: Bass Reeves
Credit: Oklahoma Historical Society Archives

According to renowned Black historian Jimmie Lee Franklin, the Black communities were seen as a "protective shield" to those who lived in them. There were several dangers to living in mixed communities in the time period immediately after Reconstruction. Opportunities for Blacks there were slim to none.

Higher Education was limited to Blacks in Indian Territory, so colleges such as the Creek and Seminole College in Boley and the Agricultural and Normal University (now known as Langston University) in Langston, Oklahoma were created for Blacks by Blacks. Langston would grow to rival the White universities of the time. Imman Page would serve as the first president of the college that would become my own alma mater. One interesting thing about Boley was that the town rarely asked for assistance from the Whites. Boley was independent.

The popularity of Canadian and African immigration was on the rise during the Nadir. Canada's reputation as a "Negro safe haven" still resounded in Black communities and when some found the opportunity to escape there, they took it. However, many would find that the racist attitudes in Canada were no different from those in the Deep South (Crockett, 1979).

The idea to organize a mass African Exodus was once proposed in Boley. However, it was not welcomed with open arms. Many Boleyites thought of themselves as Americans and saw no gains in the journey. The only outcomes they could imagine were turmoil and death.

The Boley Boosters and Boley's Successes

Photo: The Boley Town Council. My great-grandfather Milton is the farthest on the left
Credit: Our Boley Picture Book

By 1912, Boley contained fifty-four business establishments which included five hotels, seven restaurants, four department stores, and an ice plant. As mentioned earlier, Booker T. Washington came to the town of Boley to document the progress. Among the group of men who hosted Dr. Washington during his stay were a few of the Boley Boosters. "Gentlemen of Boley, Oklahoma, I am glad to meet you and to note the great work you are doing in building up the largest and best Negro town in the world" (Washington, 1908). The concept of the Boley Boosters was frequently debated, but they were no more than men who came from humble beginnings

The First Boley Town Council was created a few years after the town was established. My great-grandfather Milton Wallace had the honor of being one of the first to serve on it. Milton owned a clothing store and had several newspaper ads promoting his business. The Bowlers were also financially savvy - at least, from the looks of it they were. My grandfather James owned several acres of land

and had a successful farm. He always had a new truck every other year, it seemed, and our family never went hungry. From this alone, one would have considered our families to have been financially successful. I am honored to have two Boley Boosters in my family.

Photo: Hilliard Taylor
Credit: Our Boley Picture Book

Aside from my lineage, there were other successful Boleyites in town. Hilliard Taylor was another prominent businessman who was influential in building up Boley's commercial and industrial world. Taylor, who was originally a Texan, migrated to Boley in search of entrepreneurial opportunities. He was one of the most successful cotton merchants in the state of Oklahoma. His cotton gin company, The Hilliard Taylor Cotton Gin, had the potential to be one of the best in the nation. In fact, it had three facilities in operation. The Perry and Young Gin as well as the S.J. King Gin were also in operation at the time and experienced relative success.

Photo: D.J. Turner
Credit: Our Boley Picture Book

    D.J. Turner once had a revelation about a lucrative business that he could create in Boley. It was a business that would not only bring him success but also serve as "a much needed" business addition to the town. His family moved to Indian Territory when he was a small child and he grew up with the Natives in his area. He learned a few of their ways and even married an Indian woman when he became of age. Because of this union, he was able to obtain several acres of land, some of which were utilized for his future business. Turner took unique measures towards making this business a success (Boley Commercial Club, 1911).

    He wanted to create a pharmaceutical store, but in order to learn the business of pharmacy he needed to know the ABC's of pharmacy itself, so he enrolled in and completed a pharmacy class. He did this also in order to "protect the theme upon which his business was established," so that he would be able to employ those who were from "practical and educated" backgrounds. Turner's hard work perfecting this business was exhibited in the quality of the products sold there.

His professional demeanor was just a pleasant addition to the high-class reputation of his store. He was extremely proud of the wave of Black migration to Indian Territory because the migrants came with knowledge that was "helpful to Indian Blacks," such as cultivating lands. Turner owned a drugstore by the same name, and he owned stock in several businesses. His connections helped him become one of the wealthiest people of the time period.

W. C. OWENS,
A Prominent Business Man.

Photo: W.C. Owens
Credit: Our Boley Picture Book

Mr. W.C. Owens was a record keeper for cotton as well as a stockholder in the Boley Publishing Company. He was a Boley Booster in his own right because he excelled in organization better than any other man. Another prominent entrepreneur was Professor E.M. Watson, one half of the pair who made the Dolphin-Watson Mercantile Company a success (Boley Commercial Club, 1911).

Originally from Dallas, Watson excelled in his studies during his youth, allowing him to graduate from high school two years early. After obtaining a Bachelor's of Science degree with honors in 1904, Watson became a successful teacher in Texas before moving to Raleigh to work at Shaw University. He found himself in Boley where he became the principal of the school district before relocating to start a career with Dolphin-Watson.

Mr. L.L. Dolphin was the other half of the successful Dolphin-Watson business empire. Dolphin, also known as Lonnie, was a native of Beatrice, Alabama. He was a graduate of the A&M College where he obtained a degree in Business. He came to Boley to take over his father's business as a bookkeeper. He was assisted by his sister Bennie. Bennie broke many barriers in the business world as a Black female possessing extraordinary business knowledge.

Photo: Mayor McCleod
Credit: Our Boley Picture Book

Mayor W.H. McCleod served Boley with intelligence and wit. He was known as the "king of the Boosters" and had a brilliant flair for business. He was mayor when Boley was truly at her prime and his leadership moved the town forward in the right direction. Born and raised in Tennessee, McCleod moved to Arkansas briefly before making his way to Boley in 1907. He soon after was elected mayor.

Another business mastermind was D.C. Fitzgerald. A native of Nashville, Tennessee, Fitzgerald worked in Kansas in the 1870s before he relocated to Indian Territory in 1896. He was in charge of business transactions for the Fort Smith and Western railway. A beloved Boley Booster, he was known as "Fitz" to his friends and colleagues.

Photo: W.M. Bledsoe
Credit: Our Boley Picture Book

W.M. Bledsoe, also a native of Tennessee, was the city treasurer for Boley during its prime. After moving from the

East, Bledsoe settled in Ripley, Oklahoma before making his way to Boley. Once there for a few years, he opened a grocery store and did well in the business and his success earned him a position as a bookkeeper for Hillard Taylor's cotton business along with that of Perry and Young. Bledsoe moved his way up to being elected city Treasurer with a bond fixed at $20,000.

Photo: F.B. Jones.
Credit: Our Boley Picture Book

An Ohio native, F.B. Jones was an educator and former principal in West Virginia before coming to Boley. Aside from his education background, Jones quickly became bookkeeper for the Farmers and Merchants Bank. Possessing a sharp business skill and an enlightening personality, he proved a great asset to the bank.

One impressive fact about Boley is not only was it home to many business minds, but there were several in the legal and medical profession who decided to settle there. Some didn't have an education past elementary school, however there were many others who had a college education. This was a great mix and despite the education levels, there was a lot of talent that existed amongst the townspeople.

Photo: Judge M.A. Sorrell
Credit: Our Boley Picture Book

Judge M.A. Sorrell was another force in the legal world in Boley serving as Justice of the Peace during her prime. He was born and raised in a farming community in Fort Gibson where he gained a vast knowledge of agriculture. He went on to attend the State Normal School (Emporia State University) in Kansas and then the Lincoln Institute in Missouri, finally earning his J.D. at the Chicago School of Law.

Sorrell returned to his native Oklahoma to do business in real estate in 1905 in Vinita. He left after four years to relocate to Boley where he opened another real estate business that took off instantly. He became Justice of the Peace in 1911. Sorrell remains an ambitious young man in Boley's memory.

Photo: G.W.F. Sawner
Credit: Our Boley Picture Book

G.W.F. Sawner was a legal extraordinaire who came to settle in Boley after years of operating a successful law firm in Guthrie. His firm Twine, Saddler & Sawner was the first that was ever run with a Black attorney included in Indian Territory. After practicing law he decided to participate in the cotton business, in which he had been successful in his native Texas. He is known for being the first Black to acquire cotton on his own and also to do business with the English market.

Photo: Dr. I.W. Young
Credit: Our Boley Picture Book

Boley was also the home to several in the medical field. Louisiana's Dr. Isaac W. Young moved to Boley after getting a high referral from the state of Louisiana's medical community. Before moving to Boley, he practiced medicine for almost twelve years. Dr. Young was a skilled surgeon and, like several other Blacks in the profession, he was capable of competing with the best in Oklahoma. His vast medicinal knowledge was extraordinary and Boley was blessed to have him work there. He passed both the Louisiana and Oklahoma state medical examinations.

Photo: Dr. H.M. Sanders

Dr. H.M. Sanders was the family doctor who brought me into the world. Several families hired Dr. Sanders for childcare services, and his son eventually followed in his footsteps. A Texas native, Dr. Sanders obtained his M.D. from the University of West Tennessee in Nashville. He relocated to Oklahoma where he lived in Chandler before operating the Okfuskee Memorial Hospital in Okemah. He then went on to open an office in Boley located on her main street. He not only served Boley, but the surrounding communities as well. Dr. King was another Boleyite who served many in the surrounding communities.

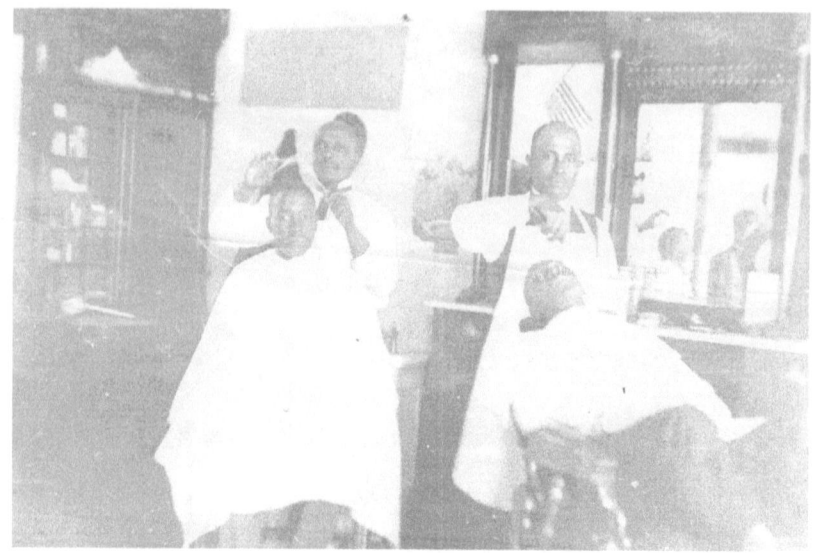

Photo: Unknown Barbers in Boley
Credit: Our Boley Picture Book

The J.N. Burnett Department Store was the leading general merchandise store in Boley. J.N. Burnett, a former cashier for the Farmers and Merchants Bank, came up with the idea for this store through his experiences dealing with the frustrations of the farmers. As a young boy, Burnett and his family settled in Guthrie. As a young man, he was the Logan County Deputy Clerk and then, later, a law clerk in the office of Brown & Stewart in Muskogee.

He obtained a degree from Fremont Commercial College in Nebraska. Burnett's business idea, much like Turner's, came as a revelation. Farmers were not given adequate profit from their work to survive. He felt that if a cash store existed, less stress would be put on farmers for trying to obtain credit as profits.

His idea was a "success and the farmers were appreciative for the advantage of doing business with money instead of mortgages" (Boley Commercial Club, 1911). The amount of money invested in this store was $48,000, and soon other goods of the highest grade of quality were sold here.

The C.L. Armstrong Furniture store was the largest in the area. A Kansan, born and bred, Mr. Armstrong's dream of furniture marketed towards Blacks took off in this humble town. His energetic nature was magnetic and his business was truly an example of Black self-perseverance.

Photo: J.C. Leftwich
Credit: Our Boley Picture Book

J.C. (John Carter) Leftwich was the founder of the Creek-Seminole college and a notable Boley booster. He was born in 1867 in Alabama. His father, Lloyd Leftwich, was an Alabama state senator during Reconstruction. J.C. Leftwich was educated at Selma University and graduated in 1890. He was a big supporter of Dr. Booker T. Washington's projects, and inspired by them to pursue projects of his own.

Leftwich also went in the same direction as E.P. McCabe and founded an all-Black town called Klondike, but things started heading into left field in the late 19th century in the South. This caused Leftwich to migrate West to Indian Territory.

While there, he founded a newspaper called the *Western World* in hopes of obtaining a political position which would allow him to help Blacks. The political aspiration did not materialize, but luckily he was offered the position of president at a college in Muskogee. This added educational leadership under his belt and led to his idea of the founding of the Creek-Seminole College in Boley.

The Ladies' Industrial Club, which included several of the most prominent women in Boley, was the oldest club in town. The Rogers and White Hardware Company was another prosperous business. Its founders were not natives of Indian Territory (Rogers was from Arkansas, White was from South Carolina) but when they arrived here, they were instant hits in the business arena.

Photo: W.A. Kennedy
Credit: Our Boley Picture Book

The Boley Commercial Club was an extremely prominent organization in the all-Black town. W.A. Kennedy was the president of this prestigious organization during Boley's prime. This organization was successful in boosting Boley's commercial interests; one year their annual sales totaled almost $34,000. Merchandise that the company handled was flour and sugar, as well as cars. Notable members included Judge M.A. Sorrell, Dr. I.W. Young, and others.

Photo: The Boley Commercial Club

Two other dry goods stores were in operation, run by G.W. Parks and T.M. Woods. Three cotton gins were also in operation during Boley's prime; those were owned by S.J. King, Perry & Young, and Hillard Taylor. Lumber was a flourishing industry in Boley. The McRiley Lumber Company was the only one of its kind in the town, and it always met with friendly competition. Mr. McRiley had been in the lumber business for most of his life and was a phenomenal Boley Booster.

List of Boley's Businesses founded between 1912 and 1934

Adams Grocery Store
Alexander's Cash Grocery Store (proprietor, Ed Armstrong)
Armstrong's Grocery and Funeral/Burial Association
Baker & Roberts Hamburger Place
Bacon & Bacon General Store
Berry's Café
Boley's Realty & Loan Company
Boley's Undertaking Company (proprietor, O.H. Bradley)
Boley's Electric Gin (J.H. Caldwell, manager)
Brown's Dry Goods Store
Dolphin's Store (Lewis Dolphin, proprietor and Bessie Dolphin, manager)
Douglass & Douglass Variety store
Fisher's Grocery Store
Hazel's Market
Hazel & Hazel General Merchandise
D. W. King General Store
J.H. McRiley's Lumber Co. & Contractor
H. & J. Jones & Brothers carpentry
H.B. Moon's Shoe Service Shop
S.A. Montgomery's Dressmaking Shop
John Owens Uptown Grocery & Meat Market
Ozark Garage (A.H. Tomlin, manager & Roland Floyd, mechanic)
R.B. Smith Blacksmith Shop
Roscoe Young Atlas Garage (C.P. Young, manager)
Smith & Morrison Shoe Stores
Sparks Variety Store
Turner's Hardware (Lonnie Turner, proprietor)
Mumford's Jewelry Shop

Other Boley Grocery Stores

Mrs. M.W. Brown Grocery
Burnett Brothers
Cozine Grocery & Dry Goods Company
Farmers Trading & Business
Glayes & Young
Hazel, Owens, & Graddy
L.N. Holmes
W.C. Love
McCormick & Sons
W.H. McLeod
B. Oliver
Issac & Hollie S. Robinson
Bell Subject
Wallace & Sons

Millinery Shops

Mrs. Ann Cowan Millinery
Mrs. N.E. Tieual Millnery

Masonry Companies

Joseph Campell
W.F. David
S.L. Morris
H. & J. Jones & Brothers

Barber Shops

E.L. Eubanks
J.A. Jeferson
Samuel M. Mathonican
C.H. Russan

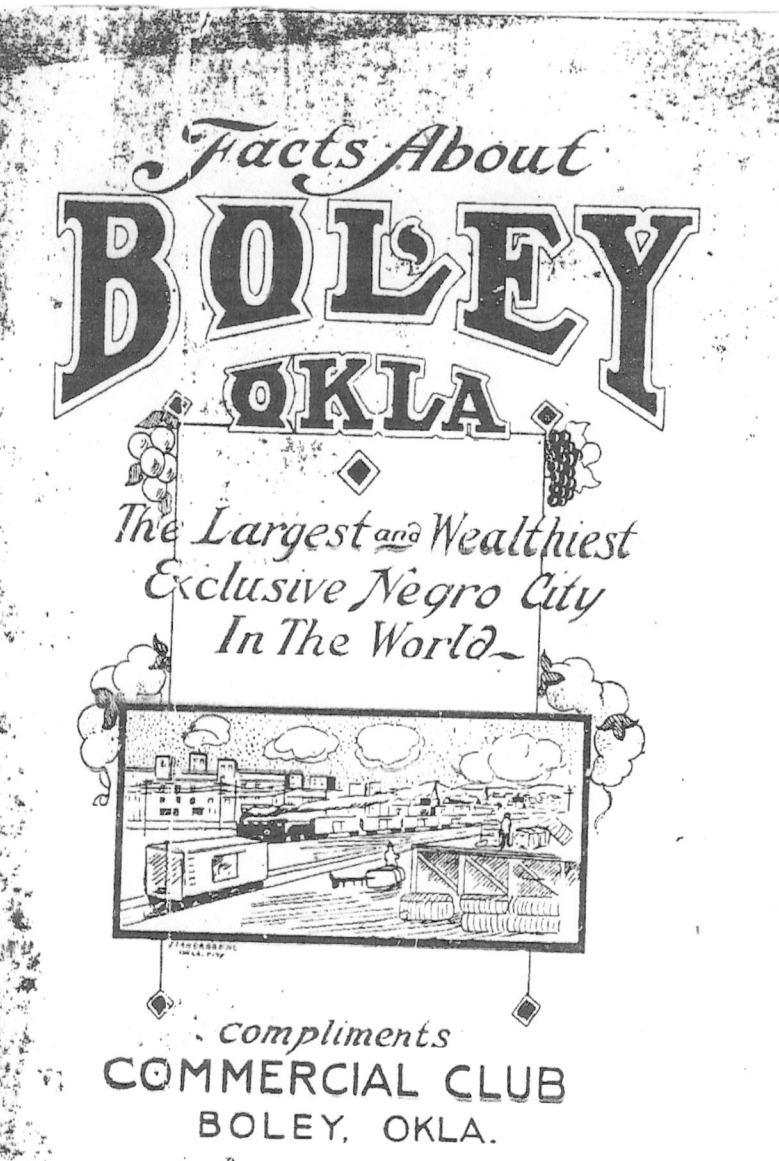

Photo: The Boley Commercial Club
Credit: Our Boley Picture Book

Photo: Masonic Temple
Credit: Our Boley Picture Book

The Masonic Temple, built in 1912, served an important role in the Boley community by housing town functions such as newspaper publishing and voting polls. Equally noteworthy was the structure of the building, which was just as magnificent as its history. Sadly, the Temple no longer stands in Boley; it was torched to the ground in the 1950s.

Agriculture was the main source of Boley's economy. Cotton was a major cash crop, at least from my point of view: my grandfather James profited from it a great deal. The Farmers and Merchants Bank was founded in November of 1906. It was also the first Black bank in America. Presidents of the bank have included J.H. Williams and D.J. Turner.

Photo: Boley Bank Slip

The Boley Power Plant came into existence in 1909. The genius behind this plan was T.M. Haynes, Boley's mayor at the time. He connected with Professor Reynolds of Wiley College, an historically Black institution in Texas. Haynes came to him for guidance about this new project. Boley was in need of an electrical generating plant, so the plan was brought to the town council. After thorough negotiations and $20,000 of funding, the Boley Light and Power Company was in commission. Student engineer workers were recruited from Wiley to help out with the company. By 1916, this plant provided electricity to all of Boley.

Photo: Volunteer students from Wiley
Credit: Our Boley Book

In 1911, Boley incorporated a municipal water system. The 200,000- gallon water tower was designed to serve Boley for over 60 years; however, it became old and rusty by the 1960s. The tower had also acquired several leaks, so by 1969 a new standpipe was created. The old tower, however, was not torn down. It continues to be an important landmark in the town.

Boley in its Prime

As a boy, I would wander with my cousin Toy through the town of Boley looking for coins to purchase candy and other snacks. In this day and age, one dollar can buy a lollypop and a small bag of chips. Back in the 1930s, one dollar could get you one row of candy and a bag of chips. Toy and I once found one dollar and felt we were the richest kids in the world. We both came from humble beginnings in our town, but our family made sure we were taken care of. Everyone in Boley was practically family because everyone took care of each other in one way or another.

Religion in Boley

Photo: Antioch Church, one of the oldest in Boley
Credit: Our Boley Picture Book

"Boy, get up!" my mother Leoneise would yell. It was Sunday and my mother and grandparents were getting everyone prepared to go to St. Emanuel Baptist Church, our family church. Like a typical kid, I wanted to stay home and play with my toys instead. In the Black church, the service did not last a measly 20 minutes; in my community it was an all-day affair. The tradition of religion in Boley is almost as old as the town itself.

Photo: Oldest church in Boley
Credit: Our Boley Picture Book

The name of the first church built in Boley is unknown, but the building itself is still standing at First and Cedar Street. It did not house just one specific denomination. People of multiple faiths worshipped here. The Ward AME (African Methodist Episcopal) Church and CME (Colored Methodist Episcopal) were in commission and had many faithful followers.

Photo: Unknown preachers in Boley
Credit: Our Boley Picture Book

Chapter 3
Boley in Print

"Boy, I want you to read the newspaper from front to back and thoroughly," my grandfather James Bowler told me every day after school. This was required of me not only because it was important for me to know current events in our community, but also to enhance my general knowledge and reading skills. My grandfather was adamant about this because he had not had the luxury of newspapers to read in his household. As a matter of fact, access to any reading materials was limited for him, so when he found an opportunity to obtain these he used it to hone our reading skills. The newspaper that he required me to read was the *Okemah Leader* because Boley's own newspapers were not yet in existence during my childhood. However, the three Boley newspapers that came out in the early 20th century were great assets to our town.

The Boley Progress was our first local newspaper, with the first issue coming out on March 5, 1911. Upon print, *The Boley Progress* contained several editorials and advertisements, including a very special article urging non-residents to visit the young establishment. *The Boley Progress* was very instrumental in not only luring attention to our town but also keeping the residents updated on Boley's latest happenings. Announcements from the residents as well as notices about new businesses in town filled each issue.

Boley Progress newspaper. Credit: Oklahoma Historical Society Archives

Boley Progress newspaper. Credit: Oklahoma Historical Society Archives

The following is an excerpt of the opening statement that appeared in some of the first issues of the *The Boley Progress:*

> The story of the glory of Boley has been told and told again. But it loses nothing in the telling; and unless for some particular reason one is interested in the progress of the city, he is apt to miss connection with the record of its wonderful prosperity; for the story of yesterday is soon old and that of today is quickly changed into a back number, in her onward march of prosperity, so wonderful, the changes so numerous the only way to remain in touch with them is to keep one eye continuously on her record of activity. Not even the Boley of today would recognize the Boley of a year ago in spite of the short space of time.
>
> *Credit: The Boley Progress, 1905*

The Boley Progress was remarkable not only for the fact that it was the longest lasting Boley newspaper, but also that it was the only Boley newspaper that existed during the transition of Indian Territory into the state of Oklahoma. Boley's newspapers focused on stories that affected African Americans while also containing news bits about events occurring elsewhere in the country. For example, in a 1905 issue of *The Progress*, the incident involving Geronimo and Roosevelt was featured on the front page.

The header of the newspaper usually contained urgent news lines such as "Go to the School Building, Friday, September 1, 1914. Important Business!" and "Ask Your Candidate How He Stands For Water Works - Then Vote Right!" The newspaper was an effective means of informing the citizens of Boley of important current events in the town.

Advertisements for businesses such as H. Taylor Gin Company and The Royal Star Barber Shop highlighted the growing businesses of Boley. This attracted many residents outside of Boley, and even White residents in surrounding towns wanted to do business with Boleyites. The first Black newspaper that came into existence was *Freedom's Journal*, which was headed by Samuel Cornish and John Brown Russwurm in 1827. This was soon followed by Frederick Douglass' *The North Star* and a few others. The success of Boley newspapers reflected not only the success of the town, but the success of Black newspapers as a whole as well as their importance.

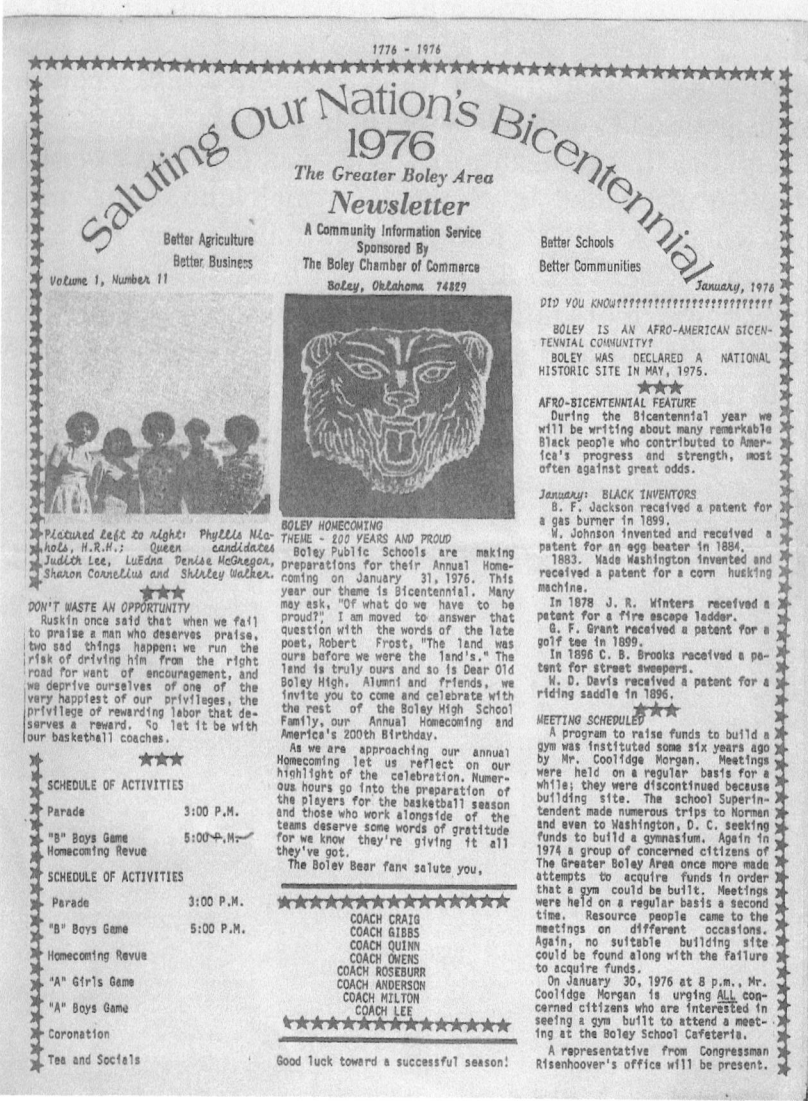

Greater Boley Area newsletter, a 1976 issue

Page 3
LADIES INDUSTRIAL CLUB NEWS
By Essie S. Williams

The Ladies Industrial Club members met in a call meeting Thursday, January 15, at 7:00 P. M., in the Boley Public Library. Madame Robinson led the devotion.

The Musical Committee chairman, Madame Spann, gave an outline of the committee's plans. They are: Elmer Davis' Chorus of Angels will be presented in a program on Sunday, February 15, 1976, at 3:00 P. M. This program will be in the Amos Temple C. M. E. Sanctuary. Each club member is asked to be responsible for at least $30.00.

The Corresponding Secretary, Madame Velma D. Ashley, is preparing detailed information for club members.

The Kiwanis Club surprised the Ladies Industrial Club with more good news. Mr. Rice reported tentative plans for giving assistance to the ladies in completing Phases I and II of the renovation project. They also have made plans to add volumes of books to the present collection. Kiwanians, we are grateful!

Mr. Charles Davis brought several volumes of books from his employer in Oklahoma City. Thank you, Mr. Davis!

MALACHI 3:10
"Bring ye all the tithes into the storehouse . . . , saith the Lord of hosts, if I will not open you the windows of heaven and pour you out a blessing, that there shall not be room enough to receive it."

The members of the Ladies Industrial Club are grateful for the showers of blessings that are coming our way.

Thanks to Mr. Gamble and his F.F.A. members for redoing the walkway.

"LIFTING AS WE CLIMB"

***

Bicentennial Year
SPOTLIGHT
By Chris Richardson

Fred H. Chiles, who currently resides in Washington, D.C., is the son of the late Fred D. and surviving Mrs. Mabelle C. Chiles of Boley.

He was graduated from Boley High school in 1935 and was in the first class of commercial Dietetics to graduate from Tuskegee Institute in 1939. He pursued further studies at Seattle University, Seattle Washington, and the U.S. Department of Agriculture Graduate School, Washington, D.C.

U.S. Senator Dewey R. Bartlett, conferred upon him the historic title of "OKIE" on April 30, 1974.

Recently, Chiles has been conferring with Rep. Carl Albert, the Speaker of the House; Robert de Forrest of the AFRO- Bicentennial Commission, Washington, D.C.; David L. Boren, Governor of Oklahoma and R.A. Ward, Director of the State of Oklahoma Department of Highways, in an inexorable effort to secure directional signing on all highways leading to Boley and the erection of additional guide signing as required to properly guide motorists to Boley.

He is currently an official with the Hotel and Restaurant Employees' & Bartenders International Union, Local #25, AFL-CIO; Vice President of the Washington-Tuskegee Club, Inc.; member of the Board of Directors, Tuskegee Alumni Housing Foundation, Inc.; a Smithsonian Institute Resident Associate; member and treasurer of the Alpha Sigma Chapter, Phi Beta Sigma Fraternity, Inc.; and a member of the Boley Chamber of Commerce.

Mr. Chiles, enjoying every minute, has spent numerous hours collecting and compiling a wealth of information concerning Boley.

The Greater Boley Area Newsletter is proud to spotlight Mr. Chiles, a truly outstanding citizen of Washington, D.C. from Boley, Oklahoma.

BICENTENNIAL - ON WITH 76
By Colleen Nixon

Through the efforts of the Horizon '76 portion of the Bicentennial Committee, spearheaded by Mr. Gene E. Hicks, Boley has had a bit of a face lifting. Street markers have been placed on the street corners, throughout the town--even on the highways.

Mr. Gene Hicks and Mr. Adrian "Twist" Green mounted the markers on posts that had been prepared by Mr. M.E. Gamble, President of the Boley Bicentennial Committee. This work was done just before Christmas, so thanks for the Christmas present, Citizens of the Greater Boley Area! Now on with 1976 for more improvements for our town.

BICENTENNIAL EDITORIAL

The Greater Boley Area Newsletter seems to follow somewhat the same format or to serve the same purpose as the newspapers in 1787. For example, a September issue of a 1787 New York newspaper might include a three-week-old event or a decision made in English Parliament two months earlier. Very much like this newspaper, some of the articles in our monthly newsletter often tell of a three-week-old event or announce something two months later. However our sole purpose is TO INFORM citizens in and around the Boley Area about what goes on in Boley and with Boley people.

"WITH BOLEY BEHIND US--WE CAN MAKE IT"

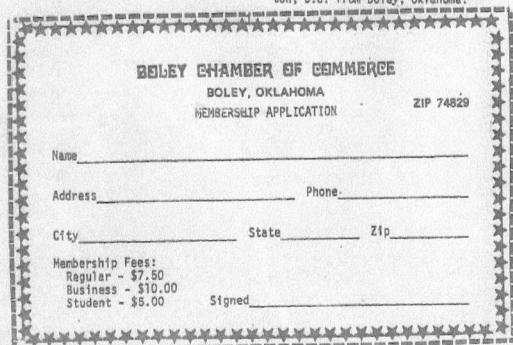

Greater Boley Area newsletter, a 1976 issue

Page 4

THE BEARS DO IT AGAIN
By Anthony Wilcots

The Boley Bears were participants in the Weleetka Invitational Tournament held January 5-10. In their first game on January 7, the Bears defeated Olive. The scoring was led by Nathaniel Quinn, Jr. with 17 points followed by Forrest Lee 14, Marcellus King 12, Alpha Roseburr and Floyd Ramsey 8 each. Others scoring were Keith White 4 and James Callahan 2.

The Bears gained a lead in the first quarter and maintained it to a score of 65-39.

Due to their victory against Olive, the Bears had another opportunity to defend themselves; this time against Liberty. Nathaniel Quinn led the scoring with 25 points, Alpha Roseburr and Forrest Lee scored 16 each. Others scoring were Marcellus King 10 Floyd Ramsey and James Callahan 2 each.

At the end of the first quarter the scores were tied at 14 all, however in the second quarter the Bears woke up and led Liberty to the finish. The game ended in a score of 71-59.

We witnessed a spectacular performance on our own court as the Bears rallied to victory against the Douglass Trojans.

The game got off to a slow start with the Bears scoring 9 points against 12 by the Trojans. At the half the Trojans were one point ahead at 25-26.

In the third quarter the Bears released some added momentum and outscored the Trojans 47-44. "Only the strong survive" as did the Bears with a win of 70-63. Right - On, Bears!!

We're proud of our Bears. They are a bunch of hardworking young men who don't like to settle for second best. Keep up the good work, Bears!

★★★

BIRTH ANNOUNCEMENT

Mr. and Mrs. Billy Aldridge are happy to announce the arrival of a beautiful baby boy, Tarod, weighing 8 lbs 4 ozs.

★★★

EDITOR'S CORNER
By Judith Lee

Now, that the new year has arrived, I wonder how many resolutions have been made, accomplished, or broken.

Why do people make New Year's resolutions; One reason is that they might want to really better themselves. They probably want to accomplish things that they didn't begin or finish the previous year. Whatever the reason, a resolution gives a person hope that he will accomplish something, even if he doesn't. It might even make him try a bit harder.

EACH ORGANIZATION IS RESPONSIBLE FOR THE CONTENTS OF ITS ARTICLES.

THE NEWSLETTER HAS THE RIGHT TO REFUSE ANY ARTICLES THAT THEY FEEL VIOLATES ITS POLICIES.

Bicentennial Year

PRO FOOTBALL PLAYER VISITS RELATIVES
By Karla Marzett

Brent McClanahan, punt returner and half back for the Minnesota Vikings, was in Boley visiting the Williams during the Christmas holidays.

While Brent was here, he took out some time to go by the Boley Public Schools and the State School for Boys to say hello to all of the students.

He plans to return to Boley to help us celebrate our annual rodeo in May. "Keep Steppin', Brent"

F. H. A. NEWS
By Pamler Stevenson

A group of Future Homemakers of America visited the Boley Nursing Home Wednesday, January 14, 1976. While there, they looked in on the bedridden patients and played Bingo with the others. Members who went to the home were: Doris Willis, Festival U.S.A. Committee Chairman; Karen Nichols, Helen Willis, Pamela Tryon Pamler Stevenson, LuEdna McGregor, Karla Marzett, Sandra Kaye Thornton and Mrs. E. B. Williams, Chapter Advisor.

The F. H. A.'ers are excited about entering their beautiful float in the Homecoming Parade.

January, 1976

BOLEVITE MAKES 4.0 at LANGSTON UNIV.
By Chris Richardson

Pinkie Laverne Alexander, a junior Business Education major at Langston University, obtained a 4.0 average by making all A's for the fall semester.

Pinkie is the daughter of Mr. and Mrs. Marvin Alexander of Boley.

Congratulations Pinkie! Bet you can do it again!

★★★

AMERICAN LEGION NEWS
By Gene Hicks

American Legion, Ward Hawkins Post #234 has grown to a membership of sixty-eight.

Buddies, we encourage your presence at the meeting of the first and third Tuesdays of each month at the hut.

We are presently formulating plans for our 4th District Meeting which will be held at Boley High School, Sunday, January 25, 1976, from 9:00 A.M. until 3:00 P.M.

4th District Commander J. H. Thompson will be presiding. Buddy Thompson is a long standing member of Ward Hawkins Post #234 and is presently serving as Post Adjutant. He is also an active church and civic worker.

With the support of the Ladies Auxiliary and Buddies of Ward Hawkins Post #234, we hope to make our meeting the best 4th District Meeting ever held.

★★★

UPLIFTING THOUGHTS

Take time to think . . . It is the source of power.
Take time to pray . . . It is the greatest power on earth.
Take time to love and be loved . . . It is a God-given privilege.
Take time to do charity . . . It is the key to heaven.

★★★

Boley Chamber of Commerce
BOLEY, OKLAHOMA 74829

To A Boley Booster

Greater Boley Area newsletter, a 1976 issue

"Happy 70th Anniversary, Boley"

Incorporated May 11, 1905

The Greater Boley Area Newsletter

A Community Information Service
Sponsored By
The Boley Chamber of Commerce

Better Schools • Better Communities • Better Agriculture • Better Business

Vol. 1, #3   Boley, Oklahoma 74829   May, 1975

THE EARLY HISTORY OF BOLEY —
By Velma D. Ashley

By 1904, Indian Territory had been divided into two parts. The western half was called Oklahoma territory and the eastern half was called Indian Territory. Boley was built twelve miles east of the western boundary of Indian Territory. The land was granted originally to the Creek tribe of Indians. At the time the town was built, the land belonged to Abigail Barnett, a Creek Freedman. It was located on the Fort Smith and Western Railroad.

The town was organized in September, 1904, and it was incorporated on May 11, 1905, by the efforts of T. M. Haynes, Hilliard Taylor and Henry C. Cavil. The town was named Boley in honor of a surveyor for the Fort Smith and Western Railway Company. Tom Haynes was a pioneer in Indian Territory as was Hilliard Taylor, and they were interested in developing an all black community to the extent that they were willing to invest their entire savings in buildings and real estate at the suggestion of Mr. Boley. Lake Moore, an engineer on the Fort Smith and Western Railroad, was interested in knowing if blacks were capable of governing themselves.

Boley grew in population from a mere handfull, the Cavils, Gladneys, Taylors, Higganbothams, Turners and a few others in 1904 to a population of 4,200 by 1915. These people came to Boley as a result of various advertising agencies. Most outstanding of these agencies were the town's paper, The Boley Progress, edited by O. H. Bradley; the Fort Smith and Western Townsite Company—a comparatively new company that was particularly interested in the growth of Boley because of its commercial importance to the company. This company maintained a manager at Boley throughout territorial days. The manager, more responsible for Boley's growth than any other, was T. M. Haynes.

The American Colony Company advertised Boley and through its advertisements announced that the company would move its headquarters to Boley. In 1905, the American Colony Company was located in Nashville, Tenn., and its advertisements appeared in the various black weekly papers throughout the southwest. The company at first planned to make Boley a city of the first class. Their next plan was to bring enough people to this area that before the territory was opened for statehood there would be enough blacks in one locality to organize a black county.

See EARLY HISTORY, Page 2

TOWN COUNCIL MEMBERS SWORN IN; WILCOTS ELECTED CHAIRMAN
By Mary Harshbarger

Members of the Boley Town Council were sworn in Monday night, April 14, 1975. Oaths of Office were administered by Mrs. Betty Lee, Notary Public.

Our present City Council Members are: Ward 1 - Sam Wilcots; Ward 2 - Amos Tomlin; Ward 3 - Theodore McCormick; Ward 4 - Isom Brooks; Ward 5 - Autry Morgan. Mrs. Leona Hall is Town Clerk, and Mr. L. G. Ashley is Town Treasurer.

Mr. Sam Wilcots, who has previously served in the post, was elected Chairman of the Council. The Council Chairman also functions as Mayor for the Town.

The Newsletter salutes all of our Council Members for their diligent efforts to make Boley an even better community for all of us.

RURAL WATER DISTRICT NEWS —
By N.W. Lee, Jr.

The lift station was struck by lightening, disrupting pump motors. This resulted in the entire station being flooded. The motors and control panels were all under water.

This situation was very critical because the lift station is located at the lowest point in the sewer system. All sewer flows to this point by gravity. The lift station performs the vital task of pumping this raw sewage to the lagoon. Being inoperative, this presented a dangerous situation. However, we are happy to report that the water has been pumped out, pumps have been repaired, controls have been replaced, and the station is back in operation. It is anticipated that the cost of repairs will be fully covered by insurance.

BOLEY SCHOOL BOARD NEWS —
By Coolidge Morgan

The Board of Education will hold its monthly meeting on Monday, May 5, 7:30 P.M., asking all members to be present.

Mr. A.B. Prewitt and Mrs. D.O. Brooks will be retiring at the end of school term.

The Board would like to say thanks to the both for a job well done.

BOLEY HOUSING AUTHORITY NEWS —
By Coolidge Morgan

A special meeting of the Boley Housing Authority will be called Friday, April 25, for the purpose of approving Harry Parker as commissioner. The meeting will be held at the Boley Housing Authority office. Pasco Johnson, chairman, and Coolidge Morgan, executive secretary, have announced that other special business will also be attended to at this time.

BOLEY TOWN COUNCIL NEWS —
By Sam Wilcots, Mayor

LAW ENFORCEMENT

An application from Mr. Donald Carson has been accepted for the position of Patrolman, beginning May 1, 1975. Mr. Carson is a native of the Clearview-Wetumka area, with 20 years of honorable service in the Armed Services. He is married, and is looking for housing within the Boley area. For certification, Mr. Carson will attend a training session for police duty as prescribed by law. This position is being funded by the CETA Program.

RESOURCE DEVELOPMENT

A grant application in the amount of $110,000.00 has been reviewed by

See TOWN COUNCIL, Page 6

Boley Mayor SAM WILCOTS

Greater Boley Area newsletter, a 1975 issue

ISSUE 26   SPRING IS HERE!   APRIL 1996

DR. H. C. SANDERS TULSA OB-GYN PASSES

By Cathy Thompson

Funeral services for Dr. Hobart Curtis Sanders, Sr., were held in Boley Wednesday, March 27, 1996 at Amos Temple C.M.E. Church under the direction of Hyde Park Mortuary. He was born to Dr. Hobart McKinley Sanders and Thelma Curtis Sanders on August 19, 1929 in Boley, Oklahoma.

Sanders was a graduate of Meharry Medical College in Nashville, TN. He was elected to the Tulsa School Board in 1973, becoming the first Afro-American to defeat a white opponent in a city-wide election.

Dr. Sanders operated his own medical clinic in Tulsa and Boley for several years and also served as co-owner of a nursing home, Sandalwood Nursing Home in Tulsa. His professional affiliations included the National Medical Association, a fellow of the American College of Obstetricians and Gynecologists, Oklahoma State Medical Association and the American Medical Association.

Dr. Sanders is survived by his mother, Thelma Curtis Sanders; his wife, Maurine Lee Sanders; daughter Thelma Sanders Clardy and son-in-law Jimmy Clardy, daughter Marie Sanders Edwards and son-in-law Benjamin Edwards; son Hobart C. Sanders, Jr.; his sister, Faye White and three grandchildren, Dante and Renee Edwards and Michelle Clardy.

NEW BUSINESS IN BOLEY

By Cathy Thompson

There is an attractive new dwelling on the Main Street of Boley. Betty and Harry Sullivan opened the doors to their new "Boley Convenience Store" on April 1, 1996. Betty states that the grand opening will be at a later date.

The store, a grocery and deli, carries those items that you always need but hate to drive so far to pick up. The store is partially stocked right now, and owners said "if they don't have it, they will get it!" Taking it one step at a time, they plan to expand to a full fledged grocery as they go.

The Sullivans have lived in the Greater Boley Area for about 20 years.

Congratulations, we are proud you chose Boley to establish your business.

TOWN GETS COMPUTERS

Langston University has brought two IBM computers to the Town of Boley as the result of a grant.

The tentative plans are to hold computer classes for citizens in the community wanting to learn.

Some of the program applications are Windows, Excel, and WordPerfect. They are in the process of finding instructors to teach the usage of the machines.

For more information, see schedule on back of newsletter.

Boley Area newsletter, a 1996 issue

Boley Area newsletter, a 1996 issue

HOUSE BURNS

By Maurice W. Lee, Jr.

The home of Larrenda Parker located at the corner of Georgia Avenue and Cedar Street in Boley, Oklahoma burned on April 3rd. Ms. Parker and several family members were in the house at the time it was burning. All escaped unharmed. The cause of the fire was unknown. The house and contents appeared to be a total loss.

The fire Department was called by Mr. Earnest Magness after seeing the house on fire. It was too late then for the fire department to do very much so the house was allowed to burn to the ground. Three volunteer firefighters reported to the fire.

Although it did not hamper the firefighters, one hydrant at the corner of Georgia and Cedar was unable to be opened. A hydrant on the corner of Pecan and Georgia was used. It was reported that hydrants should be opened at least once every six months. This duty normally falls to the firefighters.

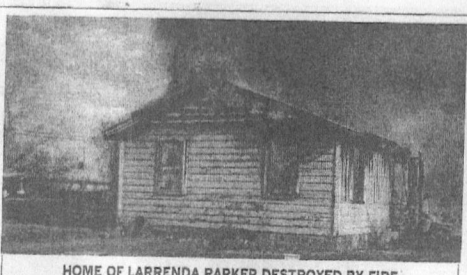

HOME OF LARRENDA PARKER DESTROYED BY FIRE

BOLEY REUNION SLATED FOR LABOR DAY WEEKEND

By Maurice Lee, III

The Boley Reunion Committee announces that plans have begun for a fourth all class reunion. This reunion is planned for the Labor Day weekend with activities scheduled for Friday, August 30, and Saturday, August 31, 1996. All activities are scheduled to be held in Boley.

This reunion is open to all with any connections to Boley.

For more information, write to the Boley Reunion Committee, P. O. Box 604, Boley, OK 74829. Those with access to Compuserve may E-mail to Maurice Lee, III, 74762,2160. Those with access to Internet may E-Mail to 74762.2160 @ Compuserve.Com.

We look forward to your participation.

IMPORTANT MEETING DATES

MEETING	APRIL
School Board	2nd
City Council	3rd
Chamber of Commerce	4th
Rural Water Dist. #1	9th
Chamber of Commerce	18th
Traffic Court	24th
Housing Authority	29th

 **BOLEY RODEO**

May 24, 25, 1996

Special Guests: Ted Lange (The Love Boat)

&

Richard Gant (Posse, NYPD Blue, Martin)

Boley Area newsletter, a 1996 issue

Chapter 4

My Family

The Shaws and Wallaces

Horace Shaw was the first documented Shaw ancestor of mine who lived in Boley, I.T. He was born in Texas in 1880, just fifteen years after the end of the Civil War, the son of former slaves. There is limited information about this side of my family and I am still venturing out to learn more about Horace. The surname Shaw is Scottish, so most likely the slave owner of his family was of that origin.

There were several other Shaws who lived in the Boley area, but through my research I have found that my family is not kin to them. Horace married Jessie Wallace and had five children: Roy, Ruby, Claude, Emmitt, and Floyd, my father.

Photo: Malissa Wallace

The story of the May family is typical of many families who were former slaves. Malissa May, my great-grandmother, was seventy-five percent Scottish and Irish and twenty-five percent African American descent. Her parents were more than likely Drury B. May, a White plantation owner from Alabama, and Louisa Lightfoot, a mulatto slave (Procello, 2004). My grandmother Jessie and her siblings were all very light-complected like their mother. While growing up I would joke with family, saying that my grandma Jessie looked like a White woman. And after seeing a photo of her, one could only agree that she really did look White.

A few of Jessie's children came to live in Boley, including Malissa, but there were some who went North and West. There were even rumors that some of those who moved away passed for White. "Passing" was a strange but common phenomenon amongst some very light skinned Blacks who came out of slavery. One who was suspected of doing this was Libby Wallace.

My cousin Kathryn Brock searched extensively for more information about Libby's story but we found that she disappeared from the census after the 1900s. We searched records online and found that she could possibly have been the wife of a successful Boley doctor, Dr. W.A. Paxton. The census record for Elizabeth Paxton matches Libby's except for the birth year, but it is a big and exciting possibility that Libby came back to be near her family in Boley.

Our research on Milton Wallace, my great-grandfather, was unsuccessful. We were able to uncover that he was born in Georgia in 1854, most likely a child of slaves, but that was the only information we could find. He was listed as a Mulatto on the census which brings me to wonder whether his father was his plantation owner as well.

After Milton and Malissa were married, they lived in Chicago for a while before deciding to move on to California. But on their way there, they made a stop in Boley. They fell in love with the new little Black establishment and never looked back.

The McCains and the Bowlers

My grandmother Zylphia's family were new to Indian Territory, like many other families of former slaves. Her mother's family were freed slaves from Alabama who had escaped to Indian Territory from the backlash that Reconstruction created. They were a part of that group of Blacks who followed McCabe's dream of the materialized new Black haven. However, her father's people did not arrive there by choice.

Irvin was the first McCain to live in present-day Oklahoma and his story is unique in comparison with the other early patriarchs of my family. Irvin came as a slave to an Indian tribe - the Chickasaws from the East. The Chickasaw Tribe (now known as the Chickasaw Nation of Oklahoma) was one of the so-called Five Civilized Tribes who were also slaveholders during the 19th century in the South.

During my research, I found that there are conflicting dates as to when he came over to Indian Territory. However, I have come to the conclusion that it was most likely in the 1840s. Irvin came with his mother Violet, his siblings, and his slave owner Tom Boyd. He moved when he became of age and married a woman named Mary; together they had several children including Zylphia, my grandmother.

Since he was owned by Chickasaws and arrived here with them, Irvin believed that he was of Chickasaw blood. Nevertheless, he had an extremely rough time attempting to prove this fact to the tribe and the federal government. Because of the racist policies of the Dawes Commission, he was placed on the Freedmen Rolls. As a result of his status as a Freedman however, he was given several acres of land from the Chickasaw Nation, and from this land Irvin created a home for his family. Yet, despite his monetary gain, he was not satisfied with this outcome and took the matter to court. Irvin would not succeed in these attempts because of a shady attorney and the Jim Crow laws of the era.

I spent almost twenty years attempting to trace him back to the Chickasaw rolls with no luck. He was easily found on the Chickasaw Freedmen rolls, but I tried to find his mother Violet in the Blood rolls. She is virtually invisible on the rolls. I hit a major brick wall in trying to prove Irvin's Chickasaw ancestry. Then, in November of 2010, I found that I had been looking in the wrong place. According to the United States 1910 Census, Irvin was listed as being Indian, but not of Chickasaw lineage.

Irvin's actual Indian ancestry came from the Choctaw rolls, according to this census. This was the biggest hurdle that he had not realized himself. His father is listed as being half Choctaw and half Negro, while his mother is listed as being Negro. Despite these records, it is not clear whether Choctaw was the only Indian blood he possessed. Even though there is a possibility he may have been Chickasaw, I have determined that it is a great possibility

Irvin was sold from a Choctaw owner to a Chickasaw. To this day we are not certain.

After researching these documents about Irvin, I took it upon myself to travel to Durant with my wife Lena back in November. I went to the Choctaw Nation Headquarters to apply for citizenship in the tribe, something my ancestor did not have the funding or support to do. I want to gain citizenship in the tribe not only for my descendants, but also for Irvin so he can have his rightful place on the Choctaw rolls. I feel that I am the last link in my family with the ability to do so since many of the elders have passed on. We will try with the Chickasaw Nation as well to rule out any other options.

Unfortunately this is a hurdle that many people of African descent face when tracing Indian ancestry. Hopefully I am able to solve this mystery so that I will one day be able to enroll my offspring. I want to do what is right by my ancestor.

Photo: James and Zylphia Bowler

My grandfather James was born in Bossier Park, Louisiana to Armedia and Charlie Bowler. Not much is known about his father but it is documented that he was an African who had the skill of rice cultivation. This is a skill for which Senegalese people were known. James and his brother worked together for a hateful plantation owner when they were young men.

One day, they became fed up with their treatment and made the journey out West to Indian Territory. As mentioned earlier, my grandfather did not have a lot of education under his belt, however he was one of the most intelligent men in the community. He was one of the first to attend different conferences on agriculture and farming.

James's sister Becky went on to Columbus, Ohio to teach school. She kept in touch with him throughout her life, as evidenced by letters we found written by her. Unfortunately, this is the only piece of history we have about Becky.

My grandfather's round trip ticket to an Annual Negro Farmer's conference in Alabama

Photo: my grandmother Zylphia with my aunt and an unknown grandchild

My grandmother Zylphia married James Bowler. They had ten children together including my aunts Clarissa, Velmastein, Alverta, and Leoneise, my mother. Alverta went on to attend Tuskegee for two years but graduated from Langston. My aunt Clarissa would go on to attend and graduate from Langston as well. My mother went to nursing school while my siblings and I stayed in the care of my grandparents.

Photo: My mother Leoneise and her sisters Clarissa and Alverta

My mother and father had three children: Sullivan, LeeEtta, and myself. We were all raised in the same community and reared with the same values. However, for some reason my mother was hardest on me. She once told me that she did this not only because I was the oldest, but because she knew I had the potential to do great things and she couldn't allow me to go astray. With added guidance from my grandparents, I was able to demonstrate these values when I left Boley.

My father Floyd went on to serve in World War II and was one of the drivers for the Red Ball Express. Several men in our family chose to serve in the military because it was one of the few opportunities open to men of color at the time.

Photo: African American Red Ball Express drivers
Credit: Library of Congress

A few of the pioneer families in Boley

Shaw

McCain

Ashley

Turner

McCormick

Lee

Taylor

Finley

Elmore

Brown

Wallace

Bowler

Barnett

LeGrand

Minnis

Chapter 5
Boley after Statehood

Photo: "Colored waiting room" sign. Credit: Library of Congress

Pro-slavery turned pro-segregation. Whites in the surrounding territories were looking for answers to their "negro" question. They had answered their Indian question with the Indian Removal Act, placing them in reservations in foreign lands. The successful solutions that the Blacks had found for themselves through these self-made thriving communities had angered Whites to a boiling point. This was simply not the answer they had been looking for. Therefore, the road to the disenfranchisement of Blacks in Indian Territory started when Oklahoma became a state in 1907.

In the early 20th century, the Democratic Party had taken over Oklahoma's state legislature. As a result, every right that the citizens of Boley and other Black towns in the state possessed was diminished. Before statehood, Blacks had held high positions in government, including E.P. McCabe, who was elected state auditor. Blacks were also more inclined at that time to vote Republican because Republicans held liberal views and had a reputation as being the party who brought forth Emancipation to the former slaves. Therefore, the Democratic takeover was especially detrimental to Blacks.

Boley's citizens were split on the issue of possibly changing parties. Their loyalty to the Republicans would create continuous turmoil for them. Their ideals would remain the same but some citizens would become more Democratic "in name only" (Crockett, 1979). They would also find the Presidency of Woodrow Wilson to be detrimental to the civil rights of African Americans everywhere.

Photo: Laura Nelson in Okemah
Credit: Oklahoma Historical Society

Lynchings were also on the rise all over the country, but perhaps the most horrific profile of this practice was that of Laura Nelson in Okemah, only several miles away from Boley. Nelson and her son were captured by a mob of angry Whites who were looking for her husband. They had accused him of rustling cattle (it is not known if their claim was accurate or not). Since they could not get Laura or her son give them information about his whereabouts they took them instead. Before lynching Laura, she was raped by the mob with her son forced to watch.

After she and her son were beaten repeatedly, they were both hung from a bridge in the town. This was information that I learned only recently, and it is still shocking to me because I had always used that bridge as a young man when I traveled to different places with family. I never knew of the horrific act that occurred there. This heinous event inspired Boleyites to spring into action for civil rights.

Chapter 6
Sand Creek Community and Boley Education

In recent years, I have become very concerned about the Sand Creek community legacy. The community in which I was born and which is an important part of my childhood history should be noted and well documented. In 2001, my family and I attended the Sand Creek community reunion. That experience brought back many memories of this prosperous place.

In 1910, the Sand Creek community came into existence. Sand Creek is a place of import to me because it is where I virtually grew up. It is located between the towns of Boley and Castle, Oklahoma. Several people have wondered about the name "Sand Creek" and its origins. The name was actually inspired by the sandy creek that was located between the community's school and F.H. Wigg's store. As this creek was popular among the residents, they therefore affectionately named the area "Sand Creek" community.

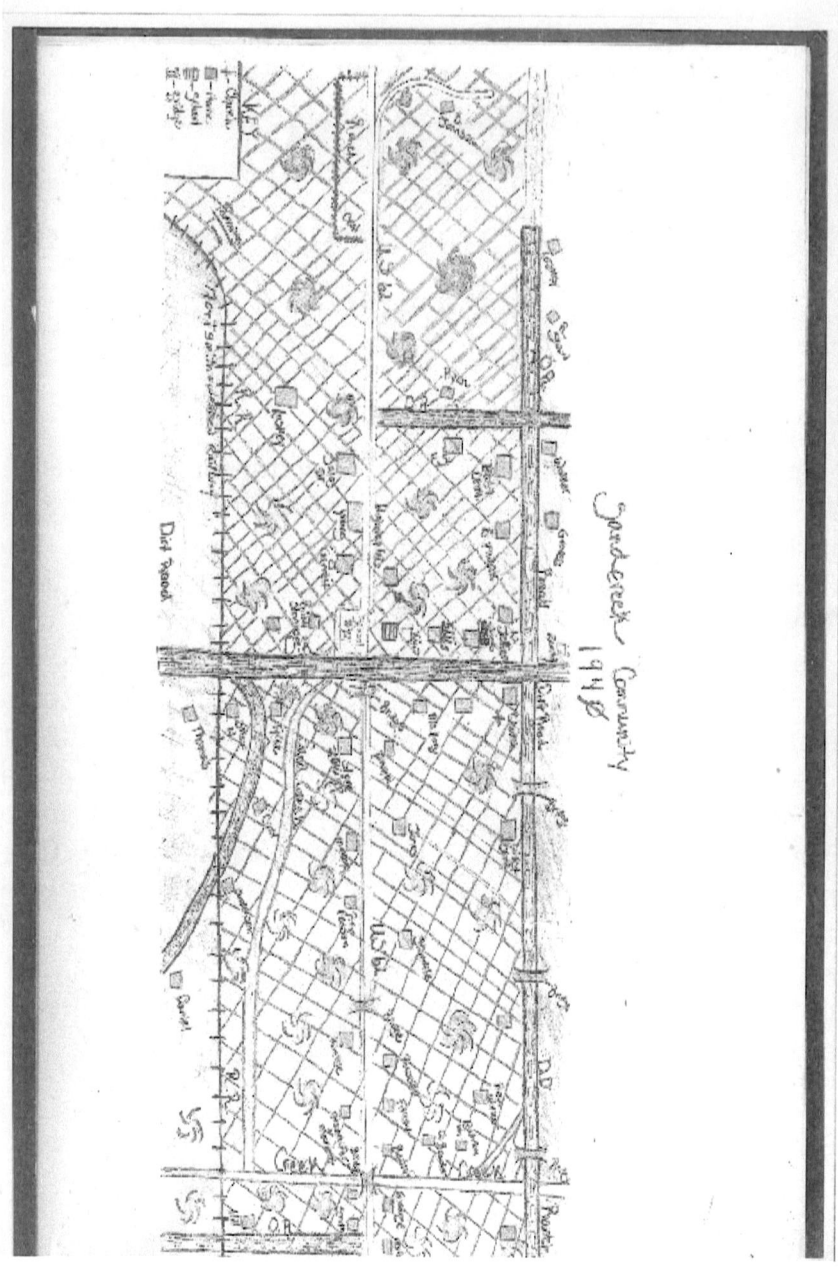

Photo: Sand Creek layout

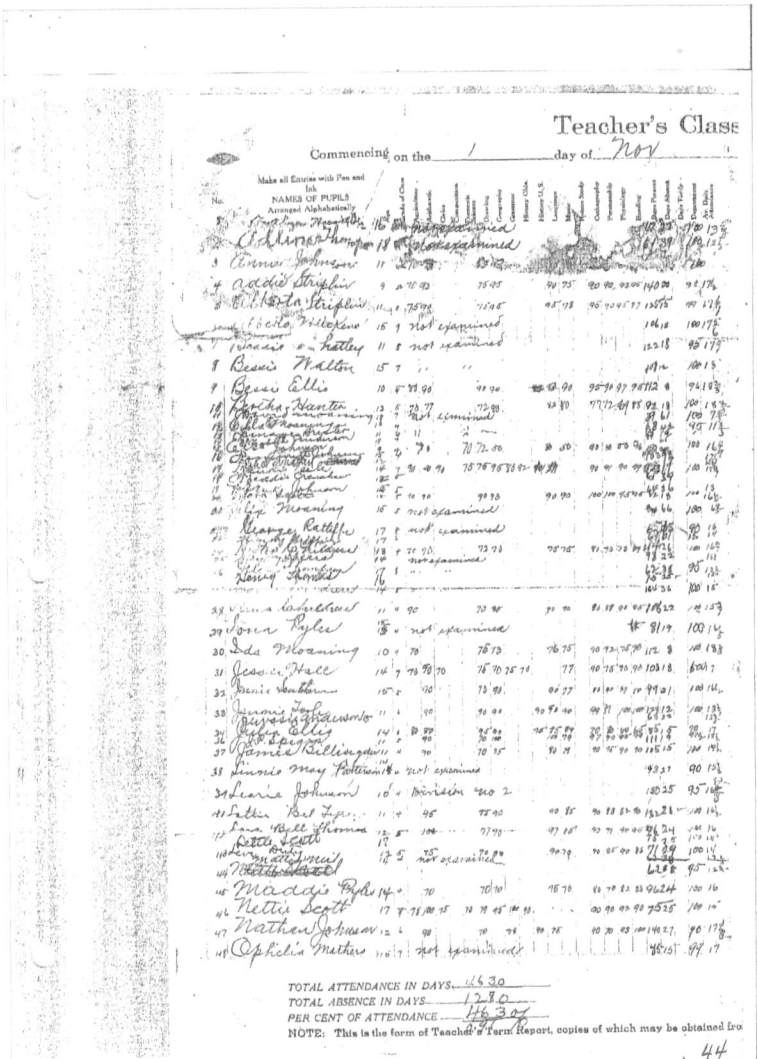

Photo: a Sand Creek school teacher's class list

In the early 19th century, when the Oklahoma State Legislature passed laws mandating that schools be separate but equal, Boley Public School officials deemed this order to be unfair. Its implementation would have had a tremendously negative effect on the rural school children because the government would neglect funding their schools.

The residents of Boley wanted the same opportunity for a quality education for their children. So it encumbered the board members to think of ways to best educate their children. There were approximately twenty-one settler families who lived in Sand Creek. Though few in number, they were honorable, powerful, and God-filled individuals.

Heads of these families were my grandfather Mr. James Bowler, Mr. Walter Tyree, Mr. U.S. White, Mr. O.S. Knox, Mr. Arthur Jones, Mr. R. Hall, Mr. B. Jackson, Mr. B. Wright, Mr. Ross Ellis, Mr. L. Striplin, Mr. T. Weldon, Ms. Susie Arlington, Mr. H. Caldwell, Ms. Isabelle Minnis, and Mr. George Thompson, to name a few. The Sand Creek community families migrated from Alabama, Arkansas, Georgia, Louisiana, Mississippi, and Texas. Through my research I found that these families exhibited remarkable endurance in order to keep this community thriving.

The first school started in Sand Creek was built in 1901. Even though it was a small log cabin with little glamour, it did the job. My grandfather James Bowler was one of the founders of the Sand Creek Community School Board. Other members included Mr. Walter Tyree, who served as the clerk; Mr. Ross Ellis, who served as treasurer; L.S. Hollingsworth; and Mr. J.C. Standifor.

The first principal was Mr. U.S. White. His salary was $115 a month. The teachers, O. Bacon and O.L. Robinson, each received a meager monthly salary of $40 dollars. Students attending the Sand Creek schools under scholastic age were paid $0.50 per month, while students who were over the scholastic age were paid $1.00 to attend school. A total of sixty-two students attended school in the first year.

Subjects taught at Sand Creek Community were agriculture, arithmetic, civics, domestic science, music, reading, drawing, grammar, geography, history, physiology, penmanship, and orthography. The humble beginnings proved to be efficient, but in 1911 James Bowler had a vision to expand the school facility.

Photo: 1939 Sand Creek graduating class

A vote of the people was taken to pass a bond issue in order to build a new school. Parents donated money, time, and materials to accomplish this goal. The cost of the building was not paid by State funds; these funds came from the citizens of Sand Creek. It took over 57,000 bricks, which required car loads of bricks hauled in by the train depot from Boley. Sand and cement were utilized to build the Elementary school. Other material included 33 ½ yards of sand. Students from primary to eighth grade were housed in this school.

One important figure worthy of mention is Julius Rosenwald, who assisted greatly in the creation of this community school through a large monetary contribution. Rosenwald was driven to this endeavor because he disagreed with the racial injustices that were being brought upon African Americans. In the state of Oklahoma, the school board refused to build high-quality schools for Black children. Rosenwald stepped in and built hundreds of adequate schools for African American children including the Sand Creek community school. Therefore the school was fittingly named "Sand Creek Rosenwald #42."

The school building was utilized in other ways too. Many community activities and functions, such as town hall meetings and banquets, were held there. In 1921, the Sand

Creek PTA was founded at the school; the group was created to encourage interaction between staff and parents. By 1924, this initiative proved to be successful as enrollment and participation had grown to 174 students. U.S. White was the principal at the time.

Photo: Sand Creek school teacher's contract

Later that year, my grandfather voiced concern about the condition of the building and a proposed expansion for a playground. Two to three acres of land would have needed to be purchased for the playground alone. He also felt it was crucial that the educational curriculum include additional subjects that were already being taught in the White schools, as this would be the only way that the children in the Boley School system would be better equipped to compete with their White counterparts. On July 14, 1922, bricks, sand, and other materials were purchased to build a new school.

Along with Boley High, the Oklahoma Normal and Industrial Institute was founded as well. An elementary school, it was founded and owned by the Colored Methodist Episcopal Church. The principal was S.H. Johnson and in 1914, the total enrollment of students was at 131. This school did not specialize in industrial work, and the curriculum consisted primarily of reading, writing, and arithmetic. Unfortunately, no financial records or books were maintained about this school. However, it is noted that money used for the school expenses amounted to almost $1500, which came primarily from contributions from the church as well as parents and sponsors.

The Creek-Seminole college was the first higher education institution founded in Boley in 1906. The land was formerly owned by Ms. L. Holloway McCormick, who was a former slave of the Creek Nation. John C. Leftwich was the mastermind behind this school and was influenced by the formation of Tuskegee Institute. The basic curriculum at the school was in Agriculture and manual training. The unique facet of this school was that it was not only Black children who were admitted here. Indians and Freedmen were welcome to attend as well. This was a plus at the time since both Blacks and Natives were discriminated against at the same accord and essentially had to build their own schools if their children were to be educated.

Boley's "Satellite" Communities

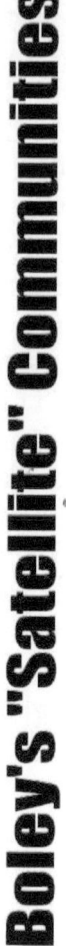

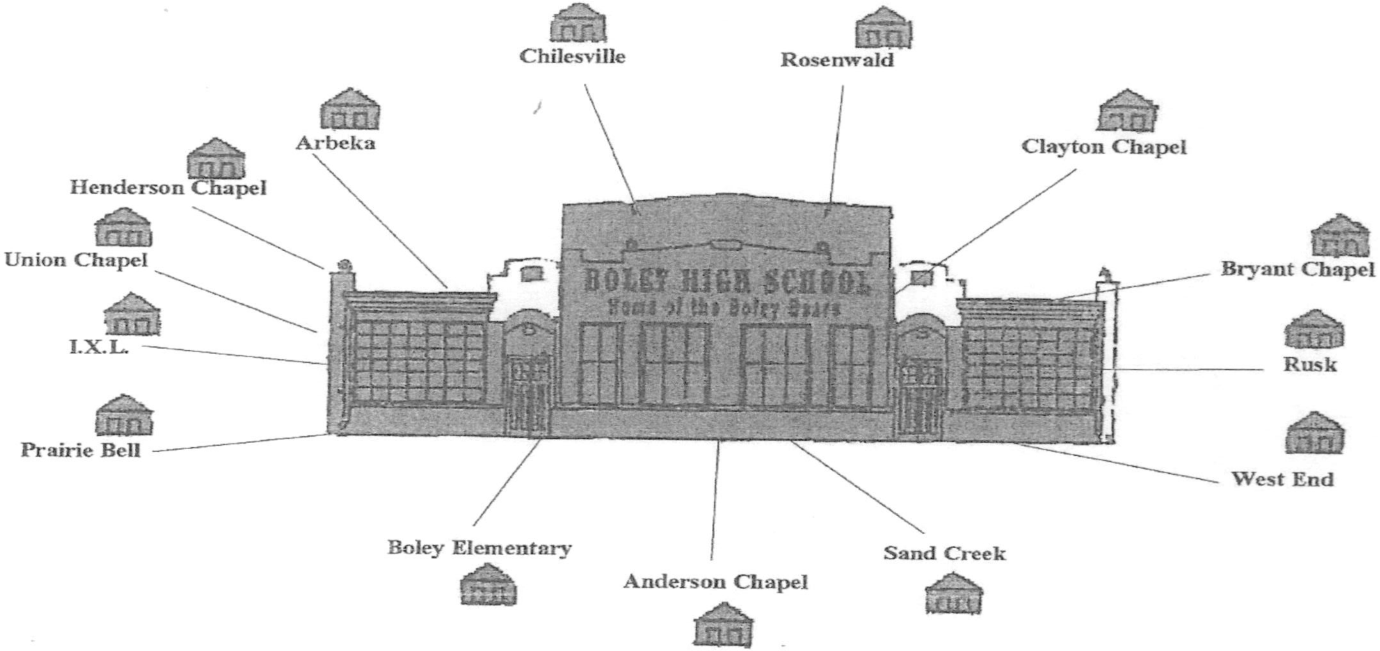

Photo Credit to Sand Creek Reunion Committee

This school would contain four new classrooms, a basement, a library, and an auditorium that was considered state-of-the-art for the time. In February of 1925, a school flagpole was purchased for $4.22. In modern times this would not be seen as noteworthy, but during the mid-twentieth century, in an all-Black community, this was a giant feat.

Several other families migrated to the Sand Creek community in the mid-1920s such as the Williamses, Smiths, Ramseys, Goldsbys, Boyds, Phillips, Caesars, Thomases, Crawfords, and my father's side of the family, the Shaws. The leaders of this community had an excessive and abundant amount of energy, and their goals were primarily focused on the well-being of the citizens and creating a healthy environment for them.

In 1930, the #42 school's principal was D. Bacon. Below is an example of the typical salary chart for teachers.

Name	Salary
S.H. Hill	$ 95.00
O. Douglass	95.00
G.W. Thompson	20.00
A.L. Langston	95.00
E.D. Grissum	9.00
O. Bacon	115.00

The principal of the Rosenwald #42 School during my time there was John N. Garrett. He was an extremely well-educated man who cared deeply about the educational welfare of the children of Boley. He served as principal from 1946 to 1960. The teachers during this period were T. S. Pann, P. Thompson, M. Hart, and A. Bowler. J. Phillip was the custodian.

Several of our Sand Creek graduates went on to college, which was a great accomplishment in our town. Bessie M. Ellis was the first in 1933. It is a great honor to mention that my aunt Clarissa Bowler Foster was the second college graduate from our school in 1938. By 1940, twenty-one Sand Creek children had gone on to institutes of higher learning and earned degrees and then forged successful careers thereafter.

My class photo with my principal, Mr. Garrett

My sister LeeEtta's class photo. She is number 10.

My cousins Franklin Hill, Orville Shaw (as known as Toy), and Geneva Standfor were also in my graduating class. We all excelled in school, but Franklin was at the top of the class. While studying at Langston University, he and I both attended a class in which the professor only awarded one A, one B, and the rest Cs, Ds, and Fs. Franklin made the A, I made the B and, well, the other poor souls in class took the lower grades.

Boley High School, constructed in 1909 with locally manufactured bricks, at a cost of $15,000. It was sited north of the present Lunchroom, facing south. It was converted into a Gradeschool around 1927, after the present High School was built. The building burned in the early 1950's.

Photo: Boley High School
Credit: Our Boley Picture Book

Boley High School was another school in the community that was later remodeled by Rosenwald. Originally constructed in 1909, it was "converted into a grade school" in 1927.

One important fact to recognize about this community is that most of the early citizens only possessed a high school education. In light of this, their respective contributions to the community were remarkable.

OKLAHOMA SCHOOL EQUIPMENT COMPANY
OKLAHOMA CITY, OKLA.

November 16, 1925.

Mr. J. Bowler, Clerk,
School District No. 42,
Boley, Oklahoma. #2.

Dear Sir:

        Your County Superintendent advised our Mr. Jones the other day that your district would probably need to issue $1000.00 or $1500.00 in bonds for payment of school furniture, etc. Mr. Jones called to see your Board one day last week, but was unable to get in touch with you.

        We are, therefore, writing to say that we would like very much to handle these bonds for you and furnish all forms and instructions for calling, holding the election and completing the issue after the election was held. You will find enclosed form of contract for us to handle the issue and will appreciate your consideration. As we did not know the amount you would need to vote, we have left that blank. You will notice that we are offering you $101.00 for each $100.00 in bonds voted, or a premium of 1%. We feel sure you will agree with us that this is a good price for the bonds.

        If your Board will go over this matter and decide to accept our proposition, kindly sign one copy of the contract and return to us in the enclosed envelope. Keep the other copy for your files. As soon as we receive the contract, will forward all necessary papers and instructions for calling the election.

        If there is any further information you desire, we will gladly furnish same on request.

        Thanking you to let us hear from you at an early date, we are,

        Very truly yours,

THE OKLAHOMA SCHOOL EQUIPMENT COMPANY
By
WE BUY SCHOOL BONDS   Bond Department.

lcp-p
encl;

Photo: one of the many letters my grandfather received for the school district

ROBERT R. MOTON, PRINCIPAL

WILLIAM H. CARTER, TREASURER

BOARD OF TRUSTEES
WILLIAM JAY SCHIEFFELIN, CHAIRMAN
W. W. CAMPBELL, VICE-CHAIRMAN
CHARLES E. MASON
JULIUS ROSENWALD
WILLIAM M. SCOTT
V. H. TULANE
CHARLES W. HARE
WARREN LOGAN
A. J. WILBORN
ROBERT R. MOTON
CHARLES A. WICKERSHAM
C. E. THOMAS
IRVING S. MERRELL
PAUL M. WARBURG
CHELLIS A. AUSTIN
ANSON PHELPS STOKES
MRS. WILLIAM G. WILLCOX
WILLIAM H. CARTER
EDGAR B. STERN

TUSKEGEE NORMAL AND INDUSTRIAL INSTITUTE
FOUNDED BY BOOKER T. WASHINGTON

FOR THE TRAINING OF COLORED YOUNG MEN AND WOMEN

OFFICE OF THE TREASURER

TUSKEGEE INSTITUTE, ALABAMA

August 29, 1928

Mr. James Bowler,
Box 127
Boley, Okla.

Dear Sir:

    Students who have remained here during the summer months are scheduled to begin registration Wednesday, September 5th.

    Alverta Bowler of our College Department will be required to pay the following fees:

```
         Tuition......  $30.00
         Athletic fee    5.00
         Board          19.25
                        54.25
```

At July 31st, Alverta had to her credit $17.67. We have not had a report on her work for the month of August, but calculating from the above, she will need about $37.00 to begin registration. This does not include books, or other equipment she may need.

    Thanking you for your cooperation in this matter, I am

                  Yours very truly,

                    William H. Carter
                        Treasurer.

C

Photo: my aunt's Tuskegee expenses

Okfuskee County
Oklahoma Public Schools

This Certifies That

James L. Shaw

has completed in an Accredited Elementary School, the Course of Study prescribed for the grades, one to eight inclusive, by the State Board of Education and is therefore entitled to

Promotion into the High School Department

of any high school or accredited secondary school in the State of Oklahoma.

Given at ~~Okemah~~ Boley, Oklahoma, this _19th_ day of _May_, 1948.

Sand Creek School
J. P. Garrett, TEACHER.   _Leona Ashley_, COUNTY SUPERINTENDENT.

Photo: my certificate of graduation from Elementary school

Chapter 7
The Turbulent Times in Boley

At one point, Boley was the wealthiest predominately-Black town in the United States. The town enjoyed a great amount of success in its prime. However, Boley did not go without its share of turmoil. During its infancy, many residents experienced harassment from Creeks and Freedmen that lived nearby. The reasons for attacking Boley residents varied among these groups, but one reason was common: they saw the new settlers as intruders.

As mentioned in earlier chapters, there was an attempt to form a "red-black" coalition, but one reason this was not successful was because of the rising tensions. Creeks and their Freedmen were removed to the area that is now known as present-day Creek Nation, including Okfuskee County which is where Boley is located. When tensions started to rise as more Southern Blacks started to move into the area, several Freedmen and Afro-Indians themselves were caught in the middle.

There were a few that sided with the Creeks (many were mixed bloods themselves) and participated in the raids on Boley. Shootings would occur and disrupt church gatherings and other public functions. This rapidly became a major concern for the townspeople of Boley, but they were able to combat it by sticking together and forming coalitions.

Photo: Creek Seminole College
Credit: Our Boley Picture Book

Those who were interested in creating better educational opportunities in Boley were welcomed in the town. The first all-Black educational institutions were being created all over the country, and those who were willing to organize successful projects were welcomed with open arms. Such was not the case, however, in the situation of J.C. Leftwich. He founded the Seminole-Creek College in 1906. In the beginning, many were on-board with this new creation.

Leftwich began with good intentions and wanted to provide the town with an institution for higher learning. However, several people came to grow suspicious of his intentions. Eventually, it was discovered that Leftwich was in fact mishandling funds. Educators who worked at this institution discovered that not only would they not be paid for their labors, they would have to find pay elsewhere. This caused several to leave the college, and Leftwich's program began to lose credibility with some residents in the town.

Food for students would be another issue arising from the non-existent funding for the school. Leftwich once expressed that "the school was organized to train minds, not appetites" (Crockett, 1979). Leftwich and his nonchalant attitude towards the situation compelled the citizens to eventually sue him. Unfortunately, the building burned to the ground and Leftwich left Boley. He went on to found other schools in Black towns and even secured a job as editor of the *Clearview Patriarch.*

Instances of prostitution have occurred in Boley as well. In the Black community, virtues were important and this act would "threaten family structure" which was "the very core of racial uplift" (Crockett, 1979). Many of the prostitutes would entertain White men traveling through Boley, and this would anger residents. The act of prostitution was bad enough to endure in society, but the fact that Black women were servicing White men was a greater offense.

Women who were caught were reprimanded by town residents moreso than the White men because women were expected to have more respect for themselves. This offensive mingling of the races even inspired some residents to come out in favor of a miscegenation law by the state in 1908 (Crockett, 1979).

Colorism was prevalent in most societies during the early 20th century, but there was one instance in Boley that left the town residents in disarray. A group of women founded a "light-skin" social club for women in the community. This move was interpreted as an attempt to create Black disunity, and the group was soon run out of town (Crockett, 1979). A blatant act of segregation also occurred. The White Way, a "Whites only" hotel, was founded in Boley by W.A. Kennedy and O.H. Bradley, two Black entrepreneurs. One surprising fact about this incident is that Bradley was a frequent advocate of Black unity and pride in the town newspaper.

Photo: Boley Bank

A devastating blow to the town of Boley occurred in November of 1932 when a prominent flame in Boley's community was put out. The Farmers and Merchants Bank had been a huge success in the early 20th century and it was incorporated into the community so much that people from surrounding towns came to bank at it. This extensive usage created all the more reason for some thugs to attempt to execute a robbery. Pretty Boy Floyd's gang were the culprits. Floyd was a notorious bank robber who was involved with the Kansas City Massacre of 1933 as well as other criminal acts.

Despite his reputation, Floyd himself did not participate in this robbery and even attempted to dissuade his men from stealing from the citizens of Boley. He knew of Boley's reputation for being closely knit and armed if trouble came into town. That was one unwritten rule in Boley: if trouble were imminent or someone felt threatened, the townspeople would be prepared to take matters into their own hands. Unfortunately, Floyd's men did not take this threat seriously.

The ringleader of the group, George Birdwell, along with C.C. Patterson and Charles Glass, went ahead with the plan. They were met with fierce resistance. When they entered the bank, they forced H.C. McCormick, the assistant cashier, to get money out of the secure vault. While McCormick was in the vault, D.J. Turner, the bank president, confronted the crooks with force and fearlessness. His brave demeanor allowed him to push the emergency button in front of the men to alert the people of Boley.

The next action would be devastating. Birdwell was livid at Turner and gunned him down. McCormick was able to kill Birdwell but his shots were too late. The death of D.J. Turner was a major blow to Boley because one of their most beloved and popular Boosters was killed by a petty thug. The citizens did not allow these thieves to escape without punishment. Charles Glass was also gunned down, this time by McCormick's brother J.L., a city marshal. C.C. Patterson attempted to flee to no avail.

D.J. Turner's funeral was attended by over 1,000 people and it was one of the most widely reported funerals of the time. He was a beloved member and pioneer in the community. He was a courageous soul who loved Boley with all of his heart and died for the sake of the town he helped build.

The Great Depression of the 1930s affected Boley a great deal. The traffic of Blacks slowed and more started moving on to places such as Chicago and Milwaukee. The success of the Fort Smith and Western railway also declined therefore leading to its eventual closing in the 1940s.

Chapter 8
Special Note on Julius Rosenwald

Photo: Julius Rosenwald

Julius Rosenwald, a Jewish American philanthropist, was instrumental in the all-black towns project. He took a special interest in the education of young Black children, and therefore created "The Rosenwald Fund" which would provide support for the renovations of the Black school systems in the South. In addition, the Fund would provide financial gifts for the renovations of several school buildings in Oklahoma in the 1920s. Rosenwald was close friends with Booker T. Washington, and together they worked to help combat the racism generated by the Southern White society and aid in the welfare of Black people.

Julius Rosenwald was born in Springfield, Illinois on August 12, 1862 to Mr. and Mrs. Samuel Rosenwald. A Jewish entreprenuer, Julius worked extremely hard to maintain the business he shared with his cousin Julius Weil. By 1895, he became involved with Sears, Roebuck, and Company (now Sears), and his wealth took off.

Rosenwald's ideology was that if the Whites helped the "negro race," many of the problems that society as a whole faced would be diminished. Rosenwald saw the plight of Blacks as comparable to that of the Jewish people. He also felt that "enough time had passed" for the "white and negro race" to live peacefully with one another (Ascoli, 2006). In 1912, he had announced that he would be giving a gift to Tuskegee Institute of $25,000. In 1913, he advertised educational job opportunities for people who might be interested in teaching Negro education. His interest in this project grew considerably in the years following.

Almost $700,000 was donated by Rosenwald for funding of the rural Black schools by 1912. Dr. Booker T. Washington worked in conjunction with Rosenwald on special projects for schools other than Tuskegee Institute, and was able to utilize over $2,100 given by Rosenwald. By 1915, Rosenwald and his recruited group went to the South to inspect some of the rural school buildings.

The first Rosenwald school was built in Tuskegee, Alabama in 1913. Despite the small stature of the school building, the cost to erect it was well over $900. Rosenwald paid for part of the project, but Blacks contributed almost $550 themselves with $360 of the funds being money saved by volunteer labor. Whites contributed about $360 to the project.

Photo: Rosenwald Oklahoma School
Credit: Douglass Alumni Association

The first school was a great success, and this encouraged Rosenwald to sponsor more thereafter. His next goal in 1914 was to build 100 schools and by 1918, funding was approved to build 300 more. The Rosenwald Fund was born.

Chapter 9
Conclusion: Boley Today

Photo: the "Boley Rodeo" advertisement

The Boley Rodeo, which was founded in the 1960s, remains a popular tradition in town despite Boley's dwindling population. People from all over the country come to see this spectacular event and Boleyites are honored to see that several others enjoy our humble tradition as much as we do. The rodeo also proudly holds the title of being the oldest Black rodeo in the country. The BBQ festival has a tradition older than the rodeo itself. Founded in 1911, it was held in order to attract residents from the satellite communities and it was the premier social gathering of the year.

Photo: Boley High School
Credit: Oklahoma Historical Society Archives

Boley High School was shut down in 2007 and the children who attended the school had to transfer to Okemah and other surrounding school districts. The last graduating class was under 30 students. This is just one manifestation of Boley's decline.

Smokaroma, Inc. - a business founded by Maurice W. Lee, Sr. - is one of the few successful Boley businesses still in operation today. Run by his sons, this company maintains profits all over the world and is one example of Boley's place on an international scale. Several businesses still exist, such as the McCormick Café which is still in operation on Boley's Main Street.

Photo: the McCormick Café, August 2011

I left Boley in the 1950s to attend Langston University, and later got married to Lena J. Hunt, the love of my life. We went on to have three children, six grandchildren, and three great-grandchildren. Despite my busy life, I have never forgotten Boley as it was.

In 2008, my granddaughter and I went to the May family reunion that was held here in Oklahoma City, and after this event the passion for writing this book came to light. My cousin Richard Procello from Los Angeles, California had written an extensive and well-researched family geneology book titled *Discovering Our Past: The May Family History, 1705-2004*. Indeed, it is because of his guidance and help that I am able to write this story about the May, Wallace, and Shaw families.

Invigorated by this family gathering, I went back home to Boley and started my journey researching more information on these families. In the process, I became inspired to try to find ancestors not only on my father's side but my mother's as well. For in addition to allowing me to appreciate how great a town Boley was and still is, it has also helped me to find myself. It has allowed me to remain content with my life as it is now and spread the word about the Greatest Town in the world - Boley, Oklahoma.

Photo: me with my sons Daryl and James, grandson Maury, and great-grandson Jessiah

Photo: my mother Leoneise Bowler Shaw

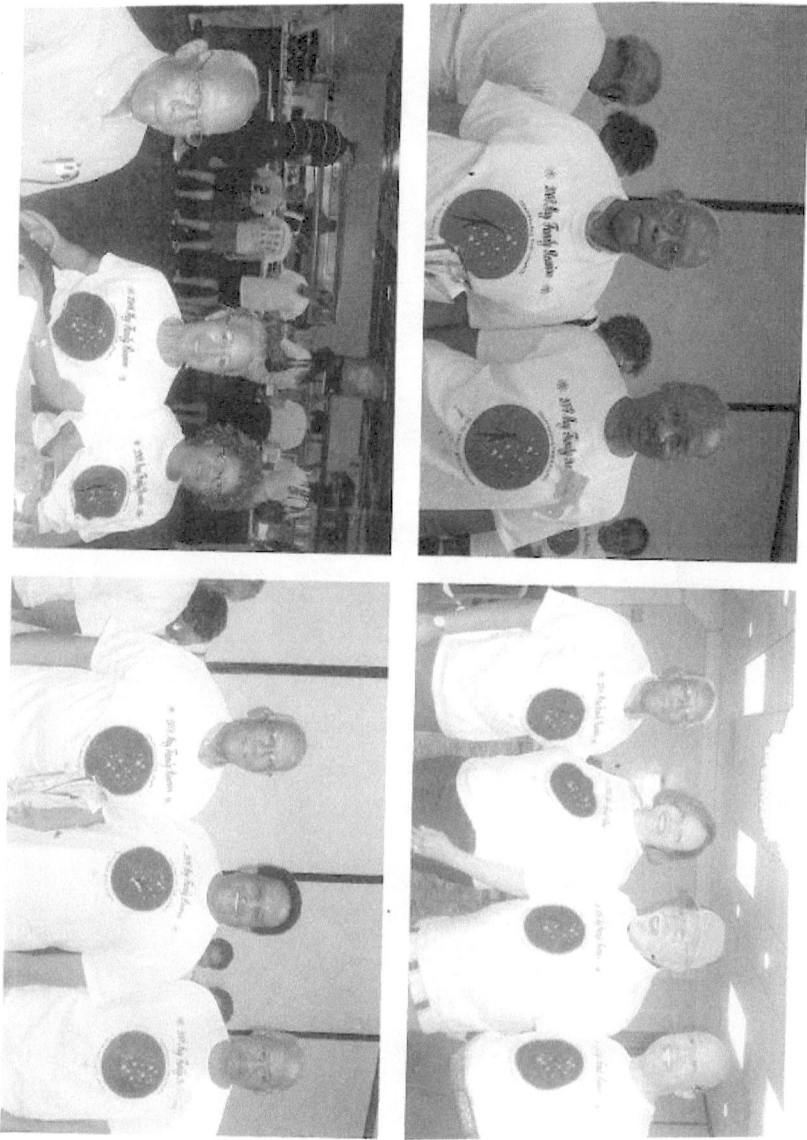

A collage from the family reuinion in 2008. Clockwise from top left: me with my cousin Odell Shaw; with my cousins I met from Georgia - they are a part of the Wallace side; my cousin Toy, Odell, and myself; me, my cousin Kathlyn Brock, and my sister LeeEtta

Grandparents

Dedicated to Jessie Wallace and Horace Shaw

Horace Shaw   Married   Jessie Wallace

<u>Children</u>   Home: Boley, OK

1.) Roy Shaw
2.) Ruby Shaw
3.) Emmitt Shaw
4.) Floyd Shaw - Married Leoneise Bowler
    <u>Children</u>
    1.) James Shaw
    2.) Sullivan Shaw
    3.) LeeEtta Lee

James Shaw   Married   Lena Hunt

<u>Children</u>

1.) James Shaw Jr. --- C
2.) hild --- Unique Shaw --
   1. Grandchildren --- Jessiah L.L. Shaw & Shi'an Shaw
3.) Marguerita Swift --- Child ---- Maury D. Swift
4.) Daryl L. Shaw ---- Children ---- Sache D. Primeaux-Shaw, Macara S. Shaw, Shakayla Shaw and Kelana Shaw

Bibliography

Ascoli, Peter Max. *Julius Rosenwald: the man who built Sears, Roebuck and advanced the cause of Black education in the American South.* Bloomington: Indiana University Press, 2006. Print.

Boley Commercial Club. *Facts About Boley.* 1911.

Crockett, Norman L.. *The Black Towns.* Lawrence: Regents Press of Kansas, 1979. Print.

Franklin, Jimmie Lewis. *Journey Towards Hope.* University of Oklahoma Press, 1982. Print.

Hamilton, Kenneth Marvin. *Black towns and profit: promotion and development in the trans-Appalachian West, 1877-1915.* Urbana: University of Illinois Press, 1991. Print.

Hill, Mozell C. (1944). Basic Racial Attitudes Toward Whites in the Oklahoma All-Negro Community. *The American Journal of Sociology, Vol, 49 pp.519-523.*

Johnson, Hannibal B. *Acres of aspiration: the all-Black towns in Oklahoma.* Austin, Tex.: Eakin Press, 2002. Print.

Katz, William Loren. *The Black West: a documentary and pictorial history of the African American role in the westward expansion of the United States.* New York: Simon & Schuster, 1996. Print.

Littlefield, Daniel F., Lonnie E. Underhill. (1973). Black Dreams and "Free" Homes: The Oklahoma Territory,

1891-1894. *Phylon (1960-) Vol. 34, No. 4 (4th Qtr. 1973)* pp.342-357

Procello, Richard. *Discovering Our Past: The May Family History.* 2004

Taylor, Quintard. *In search of the racial frontier: African Americans in the American West, 1528-1990.* New York: Norton, 1998. Print.

Teall, Kaye M. *Black History in Oklahoma: A Resource Book.* Oklahoma City: Oklahoma City Public Schools, 1971.

Unknown. *Negro Education: A Study of the private and higher schools for colored people in the United States, Vol. 1.*

Zellar, Gary, African Creeks: *Estelvste and the Creek Nation.* Norman: University of Oklahoma Press. 2006. Print.

www.ingramcontent.com/pod-product-compliance
Ingram Content Group UK Ltd.
Pitfield, Milton Keynes, MK11 3LW, UK
UKHW041958230426
12048UKWH00008B/399